CASE STUDIES IN
MUSEUM, ZOO, AND AQUARIUM THEATER

Laura Maloney and Catherine Hughes, Editors

Roxana Adams, Series Editor
1999

AMERICAN ASSOCIATION OF MUSEUMS

International Museum Theatre Alliance

CASE STUDIES IN MUSEUM, ZOO, AND AQUARIUM THEATER

Case Studies in Museum, Zoo, and Aquarium Theater
      Laura Maloney and Catherine Hughes, Editors
      Roxana Adams, Series Editor

      ISBN 0-931201-60-8 (paper)

TABLE OF CONTENTS

INTRODUCTION

This manual has been put together so that people working in museums, zoos, aquariums, and similar educational institutions might be able to move forward more confidently and armed with ample ammunition to implement their ideas for incorporating performance and theater into their programming. The chapters focus on different aspects of theater, illustrated by a case study from the writer's institution. Each chapter is then followed by a response from a colleague with potentially different ideas. The writers come from a variety of institutions, in terms of content, discipline, and size. The intent is to provide the reader with multiple perspectives on each subject. We, the editors, firmly believe there is not just one way to enter into or carry out the use of theater in museums, zoos, and aquariums.

This series of new writing is a first for the field. In 1993, the Technical Information Service of the American Association of Museums, in cooperation with the International Museum Theatre Alliance, put out a collection of previously published works on the subject: *Perspectives on Museum Theatre*. We hope that this collection of new writing will provide fresh inspiration, as well as build solid support. However, this is not the end but the beginning of a series. This collection, though broad, leaves a number of issues untouched, for example, copyright to name just one. Issues such as budgeting or technology will change again soon. Theater itself is dynamic, and because of that, we do not seek to put the final word on any aspect of it. We want to collect new writing on a continuing basis, encourage new discussions, and publish that writing for the benefit of colleagues and the educational theater community.

This publication is the culmination of many people's efforts. We wish to thank all the writers, both primary and responsory, for their commitment and contribution. The IMTAL Executive Committee provided a necessary forum for discussion. Thanks goes to the Audubon Institute in New Orleans for use of their offices and resources while getting the project off the ground.

We also wish to thank Roxana Adams of the TIS at AAM, who has been steadfast in her patience and support for this project.

Catherine Hughes and Laura Maloney

CHAPTER 1

STARTING UP A MUSEUM THEATER PROGRAM

Lynne Conner, Ph.D., Past Director of Stages in History, Historical Society of Western Pennsylvania, and Ann Fortescue, Director of Education, Historical Society of Western Pennsylvania

SECTION ONE: FUNDING A MUSEUM THEATER PROGRAM

ANN FORTESCUE

Stages in History, the resident museum theater department of the Senator John Heinz Pittsburgh Regional History Center, was developed as an integral part of all program planning for this new museum. A proposal for a museum theater program was included in fund raising for education programs and equipment as part of the capital campaign for construction of the History Center. Full funding for a resident museum theater program was secured from a large, local foundation three years prior to the History Center opening in April 1996, and two and a half years before development of the theater program itself began. This delay was necessitated by concurrent planning for facilities, exhibits and programs in the History Center.

First planned as an outreach program for community centers and schools with the goal of promoting the upcoming History Center opening, it was anticipated that Stages in History would make the transition to become one of several educational programs within the main exhibit. While the program did provide significant promotional outreach prior to opening, perceived goals of a museum theater program for the History Center evolved as initial conceptions of outreach and History Center-based programs changed.

In 1993 we developed goals for making museum theater a part of every visitor's experience by integrating it into the main exhibit. The mission statement drafted at that time included an emphasis on research, playwriting, and museum education, ". . .the Theater program will rely on scholarship to portray the ordinary and unusual experiences of a full scope of past Western Pennsylvanians for [History Center] visitors in a dramatic and enjoyable way." The mission statement provided a point of departure for discussions on the structure and management of the museum theater program.

Telephone surveys and correspondence with other museums in the United States which have theater and living-history programs brought two programs to our attention as models, Old Sturbridge Village in Massachusetts and the Baltimore City Life Museums' 1840 House. Margaret Piatt of Old Sturbridge Village and Dale Jones, formerly with the Baltimore City Life Museums and now with the Institute for Learning Innovation, were invited to consult on the program's development. Their experiences, insights, and advice caused us to rethink both the structure and management of our initial design.

The initial program structure relied on a strong partnership with a local college or university theater department. The project budget included a stipend for a university coordinator and salaries for student interns as actors. Costume expenses were not allocated, on the assumption that the university theater department would supply them. The museum theater coordinator was to be a part-time position responsible for selecting characters to be developed and for hiring, training, and scheduling the actors. Research and playwriting responsibilities were to be contracted out. After meeting with our consultants, the university stipend was eliminated and the budget allocation for actor salaries was reduced to make the museum theater coordinator's position full-time. The coordinator position also included playwriting or research responsibilities in addition to directing and producing the performances.

In preparing the museum theater program coordinator job announcement and description, we hoped to attract candidates with two of three strengths: director/producer, playwright, or historian to complement the museum education expertise on staff. We were also prepared to hire a consultant to fill in other areas as needed. This strategy proved very helpful in organizing and conducting interviews. However, job announcements in museum publications and local newspapers did not yield the number of qualified candidates (those with two of the three areas of expertise) for which we had hoped. Our next step was to contact the college and university theater and history departments, and this direct approach was far more effective. In fact, Stages in History Director Lynne Conner applied as a result of our meeting with Atillio Favorini, then chair of the Theater Department at the University of Pittsburgh.

The original design for the museum theater program called for a loose outline of historical characters that related to the History Center's main exhibit, "Points in Time: Building a Life in Western Pennsylvania, 1750-Today." Actors would perform their characters as monologues or dialogues in the exhibits replicated homes from 1790, 1910, and 1950. While the lack of detailed program design was worrisome in the planning stages, it was essential as the exhibit script was developed. This flexibility allowed the museum theater coordinator (now Stages in History Director Lynne Conner) to refine the original mission statement and mold the program structure and content to meet the needs of the developing core exhibit script and space. The resulting museum theater program, now named Stages in History, met and exceeded our original program goals.

SECTION TWO: BUILDING AND MAINTAINING A MUSEUM THEATER PROGRAM—THE STAGES IN HISTORY MODEL

LYNNE CONNER, PH.D.

STAGES IN HISTORY: A BRIEF DESCRIPTION

Stages in History is the resident professional theater department of the Senator John Heinz Pittsburgh Regional History Center. Using the tools of theater to interpret the history of Western Pennsylvania, Stages in History offers a wide variety of programming: 1) Stages in History Season of New Plays: Each year a season of original fully-staged one-act plays is offered to visitors as part of their regular admission fee; 2) First-person Interaction with Museum Visitors in the "Points in Time" Gallery: actors portray historical characters in "Points in Time" during the museum's regular operating hours. Characters serve an interpretive function by engaging visitors in dialogue about their time periods, their lives, and their perspectives on the historical events covered in "Points in Time"; 3) Monologues in the Stages in History Theater: actors perform seven-minute monologues in a small theater affixed to the "Points in Time" Gallery during the museum's regular operating hours; 4) Stages in History Adult Programming: presents various adult programs that use

theater as a tool for illuminating history, including "History Face to Face," a theatrical roundtable featuring fictional historical characters in conversation with a contemporary scholar and "Pittsburgh's Theater Legacy," an ongoing lecture series featuring reconstructed performances by the Stages in History company; 5) School Group Programs in the History Center: actors present historical characters as a regular part of school group visits. Since 1996, SIH characters have given presentations to more than 1000 school groups at the History Center; 6) History Center After-school Theater Program: an eight-month curriculum brings middle school students to the History Center one afternoon a week to explore local history using the tools and techniques of theater. Over the school year, students research, write, perform, and produce two major theater pieces based in local history; 7) Outreach School Programs: actors present historical characters at primary and secondary schools in Western Pennsylvania; and 8) Outreach Community Programs: actors present historical characters at community functions.

FIVE STEPS TO BUILDING A MUSEUM THEATER PROGRAM

STEP ONE: WHOM TO HIRE?

From its inception, Stages in History has been guided by two basic principles: a) that a good museum theater program must be based in solid, professional theatrical standards; and b) that the tools of theater, when creatively used, can be an extremely successful method for interpreting, teaching, and sharing history. I was hired in the fall of 1995 to create a resident theater program for the spring 1996 opening of the Senator John Heinz Pittsburgh Regional History Center, a new 160,000 square foot facility located in downtown Pittsburgh. Though I had never worked in the museum industry, as a theater historian and a working playwright and director, the notion of combining theater and history in a museum setting seemed natural and appealing to me. From its origins, drama has sought to interpret civic history, both recent and ancient (think of the setting for most of the extant Greek drama, for example). The inverse is also true, as contemporary historiography reveals: historians throughout time have routinely used dramatically drawn narratives to tell the "story" of a given history by identifying heroes and villains and by fleshing out the scenic background of a historical event.

As historian and playwright, director and actor, I have experience and respect for both the job of the historian and the job of the professional theater artist. I took the position because I was assured that the executive director and the director of education were committed to the idea of professional theater. In turn, my standing as a published historian and adjunct faculty member at the University of Pittsburgh assured them that I was a seriously trained historian committed to the standards of professional historiography. This combination of historian and theater professional is not unique. Most graduate programs in theater history will produce fully trained historians who have plenty of practical theater experience.

STEP TWO: BASIC BUILDING DESIGN NEEDS

If possible, the program designers should be thinking about appropriate performing spaces from the start of the exhibit design process. When I first saw the History Center's main exhibit, "Points In Time," during the late stages of construction, I was overcome by its dramatic appeal and by the performance potential of the space.

Structured around the full-scale facades of three homes, the exhibit takes a personal, narrative-driven approach to chronicling Pittsburgh's development. Further, designed into the exhibit were a series of kiosk spaces with sound barriers and seating. Though these kiosks were original designed for teachers and docents, I immediately saw the theatrical potential and designated one centrally located kiosk as a kind of amphitheater for the Stages in History company. Taking up residence in this small theater has allowed the actor-historians to perform formal monologues right in the flow of the exhibit but away from the noise and traffic patterns. Visitors are then given the choice of sitting down for a seven-minute performance or continuing on.

STEP THREE: RESEARCH AND SCRIPT WRITING

My original job description called for me to create a group of historical characters for residence in the new History Center's permanent exhibit, "Points in Time." Since our goal was to interpret the human dimension of the exhibit, we looked for historical figures and composite types with personal narratives containing dramatic potential. We also felt the mandate to flesh out the exhibit and to be demographically diverse. Since 1996, I have researched and "written" over twenty Stages in History characters, some historical, some composite (that is, fictional). All of them lived in Western Pennsylvania between 1799 and 1996. A few are famous, like Andrew Carnegie, Stephen Foster, and Billy Eckstine. Most are not famous, even to the average Western Pennsylvanian: they are civic leaders, reformers, recent immigrants, housewives, laborers, and pioneers. They cover a range of ethnicities, religions, and economic classes.

During the research phase, I consulted with History Center curators, historians, and educators, as well as conducting my own research in our extensive archives. The richest source material for creating these characters came from personal papers in the collection: letters, diaries, business contracts, household account books, and photo albums. I also have routinely used microfilm of contemporary newspapers, since they are a veritable treasure chest of information about daily life in the region. Several of our local libraries have exhaustive microfilm collections of area newspapers.

My first scripting step is the creation of a character file for use by the actor-historian playing the role. Included in the file are an annotated character biography sheet, a bibliography, and photo-copies of selected primary and secondary reading material. I try to keep the biography sheet within ten pages, highlighting the character's chronology and critical moments. I also outline suggested "talking points"—areas of potential conversation between the character and the visitor. I choose primary and secondary reading that complements and fleshes out the biography sheets and talking points. In addition, the actor-historian is asked to read selected materials from the bibliography.

The second scripting step is writing the monologue that accompanies each Stages in History character. In creating these short plays, I feel obliged to adhere to the standards of good history and to create good theater. I do this by making sure that the monologues are historically accurate, with the dates, names, and events solidly documented. Then, from among these facts, I look for a point of departure that has the potential for good theater. Does the character's life contain a moment that can be told dramatically—with high emotion and a rise and fall of action built into the script? These moments do not have to be historically momentous, at least not in the conventional sense. In fact, in many ways the most dramatic scripts are the ones that treat daily life as momentous. For example, in his monologue, the character of Andrew Carnegie does not recount his infamous battle with Henry Clay Frick over control of the Carnegie Steel Company. He talks, instead, about his relationship with his father, in particular, one night in the late 1850s when the balance of power between father of son shifted forever and left an indelible mark on Carnegie's character. These personal transitions are the fodder of good theater, and a well-trained playwright should be able to identify them and use them effectively, no matter how short the script.

STEP FOUR: CREATING A RESIDENT ACTING COMPANY

The members of the Stages in History company are all regular part-time employees at the History Center holding the title of "actor-historian." Since Stages in History is a professional theater company, we look to hire well-trained actors who demonstrate the capacity to become good historians. Most of our company members have a Master of Fine Arts degree in acting performance, plenty of teaching experience, a strong humanities and liberal arts background, and an interest in history. There have been a few exceptions. We have a long-standing company member who was a high-school history teacher for thirty years before taking early retirement and becoming an actor. Another company member is currently a high-school history teacher. It is important to note, however, that all of our actor-historians come into the program with substantial performing experience in the professional theater community here in Pittsburgh.

In auditioning actors, we look for people who are interested in the kind of performing environment that we provide. They must be experienced in improvisational techniques, they must have good "people skills," they must take pleasure in one-on-one interactions, and finally, they must be able to see the value of participating in a nontraditional theatrical mode. Some actors are wonderful on the stage, under heavy lighting, and clearly separated from the audience, but fall apart when asked to perform in a noisy gallery. Other actors are good on script, but cannot engage in a convincing "first-person" conversation.

Once an actor-historian has been hired, the training process is divided into three stages. In the first stage, the actor-historian is asked to tour History Center exhibits, observe other Stages in History actor-historians at work in the galleries, study the character file that accompanies the person the actor has been hired to portray, and read selections from the character bibliography. In the second stage, the actor-historian meets with me to go over the biographical material, ask questions, and begin to sculpt the physical qualities of the character. (During this period, the actor-historian will also attend costume fittings with the costume designer.) Toward the end of this process, I "role play" a variety of types of History Center visitors to give the actor-historian some experience in first-person interaction. And in the third and final stage, the actor-historian rehearses the scripted monologue with me while also testing out the character in the galleries by participating in some first-person interactions. In this phase I am always present, watching, listening, and then giving performance notes and suggestions when we are back in the rehearsal area. The last step is to introduce the character monologue during the normal performance hours. By this time, the actor-historian is usually ready to go it alone.

STEP FIVE: UNDERSTANDING THE GOLDEN AND SILVER RULES

From the beginning, the Stages in History company has had a Golden Rule and a Silver Rule. The Golden Rule has been strictly enforced: never make up facts and never pretend to know something you don't know. The Silver Rule has proven to be more problematic: never break character. In the first case, it is obviously paramount that the actor-historians do not play fast and loose with historical fact. I give the company members permission to say to a visitor, "I don't know the answer to that question." I also ask them to use those embarrassing moments as the impetus to find out the answers later on.

In the second case, over the last two years we have had to expand our definition of staying in character to fit the changing needs of the History Center. In the original design, docents were to be stationed in "Points in Time" to greet visitors. In reality, often the only staff person in the main exhibit is the actor-historian. As a result, we have gradually taken over the job of greeting visitors as they enter the exhibit. We attempt to do this in a theatrical manner, but of course the actor-historian must leave his or her character's own point in time in order to advise visitors on how to proceed through the gallery. We also must break character when a visitor needs to know where the bathroom or the exits are.

We do not break character, however, to answer questions related to exhibit content out the actor's specific time frame or to chat with visitors curious about our training as actors. This is an important rule, because we have found that the minute an actor-historian breaks character to explain something in the exhibit, he or she moves from the role of performer to the role of docent. This then becomes an impossible situation, wherein the actor-historian tries desperately to have a foot in two worlds and as a result fails miserably in both. On the other hand, if a visitor seems genuinely confused about the fact that we are pretending, we will try to help them understand our role by stressing that we live in a specific year, not in the year 1998. Senior citizens sometimes have a problem understanding the theatrical conceit, even with characters dressed in eighteenth and nineteenth-century garb. Since it is not our goal to confuse or to embarrass our visitors, we sometimes have to resort to winks and nudges to get the point across.

COMPONENTS OF MAINTAINING A THEATER PROGRAM

Since the spring of 1996, Stages in History has grown from a program component of the Education Division into a full department with two full-time employees, six regular part-time actor-historians, and a number of contract actor-historians who work for limited periods of time. Our programming has expanded from providing historical and composite characters for the exhibits to producing a season of original plays and offering school programs, outreach programs, lecture series and marketing appearances. Stages in History's success is based on high quality work that appeals to History Center visitors, outside funders, and community partners.

CREATING PARTNERSHIPS

When I came to the Historical Society one of my duties was to create a relationship with a local university or college theater department. Since I was at that time teaching graduate-level courses in the Theater Department at the University of Pittsburgh, it was a relatively easy marriage to arrange. The resulting partnership featured two programs: an acting internship in which Masters of Fine Arts acting candidates at Pitt served terms as members of the Stages in History company and an orientation workshop that introduced graduate students to the material resources housed at the History Center. Although the relationship was successful, it ended when the University of Pittsburgh downsized the theater department and dissolved the MFA acting program last fall.

Other partnerships have emerged in the last two years, including Stages in History's relationship with Gateway to the Arts, a local presenting organization that markets and books performing arts programs in area school districts. With Gateway to the Arts, we have been able to reach a far wider market and to expand our outreach programming considerably, thus increasing the program's visibility and contributing to the revenue stream associated with the Stages in History department.

FINDING AND MAINTAINING CORPORATE AND FOUNDATION SUPPORT

The way to find and maintain corporate and foundation support is to make sure that the theater program is visible in the community. At the History Center, I have worked closely with the marketing and public-relations staff both to publicize Stages in History programs and to help market the History Center in the community. A convincingly attired historical character is the most likely choice for a photographer or cameraman or reporter sent to cover an event. As a result, Stages in History characters have been featured in area newspapers and magazines on a regular basis. I have made it my business to respond quickly to last-minute requests for Stages in History appearances at a wide range of History Center functions, from having Andrew Carnegie ready to pose with the Governor of Pennsylvania to sending off our 1909 baseball character to the local sports stadium during a Pittsburgh Pirates news conference. In order to do this, however, it is necessary to have a staff of actor-historians who are flexible, enthusiastic, and loyal to the program.

MAINTAINING A COMPANY OF GOOD ACTORS

In order to maintain the Stages in History acting company, we have adhered to the following: the actor-historians are paid a good hourly wage; the actor-historians are paid for all their time, including rehearsals and study periods; and the actor-historians are treated as part of the History Center team and are valued by all members of the institution. In addition, we have a flexible work schedule that accommodates everyone. For example, the actor-historians have a regular weekly schedule, but they know that I will do my best to grant them time off for last-minute auditions, commercials, and film opportunities. In return, the actor-historians do their best to respond to my last-minute requests for History Center special appearances.

THE BOTTOM LINE: BE FLEXIBLE

In retrospect, I think one of the most important components to the success of Stages in History has been our willingness to learn and to change the way we operate to fit the changing dynamics of the History Center. We've adjusted in a hundred ways: from altering performance times and places to fit unexpected visitor patterns to finding the money to construct a costume stock (a major expense that was not originally budgeted for but was absolutely necessary to the success of the program) to accepting the fact that we have to tell people where the bathrooms are located. Mostly, though, we've learned that people don't always respond the way we want them to respond. We've been very surprised, for example, to see how the process of opening up our visitor's emotional lives has also, at times, opened up the more negative aspects of personal expression. We envisioned the Stages in History program as a way to teach tolerance. But, sometimes we get the opposite—racism, anti-Semitism, and sexism. Because Stages in History actor-historians reveal their character's emotional lives, visitors often see them as "safe" havens and as confessors. When that intimacy provokes racist feelings, it can be very difficult for the actor-historians. Still, these kinds of emotional outbursts come as a natural result of the History Center's mission and mandate to interpret differing points of view. The dialogue that accompanies those diverse perspectives is testimony to the power and value of the Stages in History museum theater program.

RESPONSE TO *Starting A Museum Theater Program*

DIANE GARDINER
DIRECTOR OF EDUCATION, OLD MELBOURNE GAOL

Chapter 1 provides a succinct and informative description of how Conner and Fortescue initiated and developed their museum theatre program, with practical ideas and suggestions on maintaining such programs.

The essay is a timely reminder that though museum theatre may often be started in an ad hoc manner by some

museums, it is obvious that for it to succeed and have the impact it deserves, it is essential to carefully plan and integrate all aspects of its development into the museum's existing structure. At the Western Pittsburgh History Center, Fortescue began by intergrating the museum theatre program into the main exhibition mission statement. She used consultants from other successful historic sites during the museum program's evolution. Their experiences in these sites led to important changes in the Pittsburgh program.

Conner discussed the need for solid professional theatre standards. Theatre when used creatively can be a superb method of interpreting, teaching, and sharing history. Quite complex concepts and theories can be communicated in a memorable and enjoyable way.

Conner outlined five steps to building a museum theatre program. In her first step regarding whom to hire, she says that in the United States, a combination of trained historian and theatre professional is optimum. I think this combination of skills may not be as common in other countries. However, it is a wonderful avenue to explore and encourage. Obviously, who is hired is crucial to the success of any museum theatre program. She discussed this quite fully as well as the extensive skills base that her museum requires and expects in their actors.

Conner goes on to recommend that performing spaces should be incorporated into the original design process of an exhibition. However, in my own experience this may be limited by the restrictions imposed by an historic building.

Next, she described the various sources she used for research. Historic sites, I think, are very fortunate as they suffer from an excess of suitable stories to dramatise. Her actors are given a detailed character file to read consisting of primary and secondary sources. It is essential that actors in these situations know not only a script but answers to curly questions that visitors inevitably will hurl their way.

Conner's golden and silver rules state that actors should never make up facts. Never breaking character is more complicated, but vital. As most museums who have used first-person interpretation realise, questions such as, Where's the toilet? and such, have to be acknowledged and dealt with. However, breaking role and explaining something is fraught with problems. The actor is crossing over into a docent role and this does not work.

Conner emphasised the importance of museum theatre programs working closely with the marketing and public-relations departments if they are to maintain their success. The directors of my museum changed their attitudes to museum theatre and took it seriously when visitor numbers were increased as a direct spin-off from the marketing and the high profile of the performances.

Conner discussed how important it is to maintain good actors. This can be done by paying them for the time involved in their research, study, and character development. Above all is the need to be flexible.

As an institution grows and develops, so must the theatre program adapt to changes within the building, visitor numbers and flow, and other ever-changing needs of the site.

Museum theatre provides a wonderful opportunity to express ideas of tolerance, understanding, and other ideals. However, it will not necessarily change the world overnight, and indeed, it may make no impact on an individual's ideas. Yet, it at least provides a forum to express a variety of viewpoints that may not occur otherwise.

All these suggestions are an excellent guide that can give someone contemplating using museum theatre a taste of what to expect. However, if they are truly serious and interested, Catherine Hughes' new book, *Museum Theatre*, provides more detailed and practical advice.

CHAPTER 2

PLAYWRITING FOR MUSEUMS OR:
HOW TO MAKE A DRAMA OUT OF SLIME MOLDS

Jon Lipsky, Associate Professor, Boston University, and playwright, Museum of Science, Boston

I could say: writing for museums is an art that is designed to drive playwrights crazy. The playing time is usually limited to 15 or 20 minutes. The actors are often still learning their trade. The audience can usually get up at any time and walk out. And the script has to be equally suitable to restless eight-year-olds, tired middle-agers, and impatient older folks. The lighting is limited, the sound often horrendous, and if there's a budget for props and scenery (no less a stage manager) you are very lucky.

Or I could say:

Mike Alexander, Manager of Public Programs and Science Theater, called me into his office the other day, handed me a yellow legal pad, and said he had another play for me to write. I thought: great, I like working for the Museum of Science and I need another gig; wonder what Mike's got up his sleeve this time?

> *Bogs,* he said.
>
> *Beg your pardon,* I said.
>
> *Bogs.*

The word hung in the room like a leaky balloon.

> *Bogs? What about bogs?* I said.

For a minute I thought this was some sort of code word, or maybe a curse, like a variant on "bugger!"—"Oh, bogs!"

But no, with a resigned sort of sigh that could only mean Mike was not totally happy with the assignment himself, he averred:

> *That's what the play has to be about—bogs.*
>
> *Oh, yes, I see, of course: bogs,* I said, looking down on my nice clean, yellow pad, wondering whether it would be supportive or rude to write B O G S!!! in big letters at the top of the page.
>
> *And just what do you want me to do with "Bogs,"* I asked.
>
> *Make them irresistible,* he said.

So, I could say either of these things but neither of them is strictly true. Playwriting for museums, despite its difficulties and peculiarities, rarely drives me crazy, and the real conversation with Mike about the bogs play bore only a superficial resemblance to the one I just described here. It reflects how I was feeling, and not what was actually said. While both paragraphs hold an essential truth, in both cases I reshaped the information for one reason: I wanted to get your attention.

Getting your attention and reshaping the truth. That in a nutshell is what playwriting for museums is all about. Making you stop, look, and listen. And making you think. Finding a form that will be both entertaining and informative. Molding the material so that it feels interesting, important, and relevant. Whatever we do as playwrights, whatever form it takes, has to capture the imagination of the public and contribute something to their experience. If it doesn't do both of those things in equal measure, then it not only fails on its own terms, but actually interferes with the primary pleasure of museum-goers, which is to roam. Anything that attempts to stop their roaming, even for a short amount of time, must be held to a high standard.

The high standard is this: does the drama give a human face and a human heart to the information being considered. Facing the information glut in any good museum, zoo, or aquarium, the job of the dramatist is to help the audience stop to consider a particular topic in a way that will have an emotional impact on them. The drama should help focus the audience's roaming, so that they have a better idea why a certain topic or exhibit deserves their attention. It is a way of reaching out to them and saying: "Hey! Listen! This is really something! Let me tell you about bogs!"

The Ten Commandments of Museum Theater are:
Thou shalt not be boring
Thou shalt not be boring

Thou shalt not be boring
Thou shalt not be boring
Thou shalt not be boring
Thou shalt not be boring
Thou shalt not be boring
Thou shalt not be boring
Thou shalt not be boring
And:
Thou shalt always deliver the information.

So how do we do this—not be boring and deliver the information? Obviously, the answer to this is going to change with the territory. There is no formula, no prescription for the well-made museum play. The form has to come out of the content, and vice versa.

Each job is different: the Leonardo da Vinci exhibit wants a play to sum up Leonardo's achievement; a public television station wants a play to promote interest in a television series about science and technology in the 20th century; or the education department wants a play about U.F.O.s to create a forum for talking about pseudo-science and scientific thinking.[1] Often the idea for a play will be generated more by a pedagogical need than a dramatic impulse. And it is the job of the playwright to find the not-boring, information-delivering drama in it.

The bogs play was a particularly good example of how the form follows the content. Many (but not all) play ideas come from some dramatic kernel within a given topic. In an exhibition about the rain forest, the job was to highlight the life and work of Chico Mendes, a rubber tapper who worked to save the rain forest but was gunned down for his politics. This is a particularly dramatic idea. But the bogs play came more out of a sense that the bogs exhibit needed some kind of spicing up, human touch, emotional oomph. The planners also needed something that would focus on Irish bogs, for which they had no artifacts. No obvious dramatic idea leapt to mind.

So to find the drama and discover the form, I set about listening to everyone involved tell me what was neat about bogs. Sort of like a Hollywood pitch job in reverse—I was asking the producers to sell the writer on the topic rather than the other way around. And the producers—the exhibit planners and the education department—came up with a long list of why bogs are the cat's meow: they have great things buried in them, great things growing in them, great stories, myths, and poems written about them. But still there was no dramatic form to hold these things together.

But then one of the exhibit planners showed me a photograph of a beautiful, barefoot, golden-haired colleen carrying a basket of turf dug out of an Irish bog, and the structure for the play fell into place. I fell in love. I wanted to know all about her. So, the play would be her story: the bog seen through her eyes. Suddenly a form emerged, a collage of images, impressions, and stories that might have been in her mind: images of long-preserved mummies, the myths of the boggy man, the flowering heather, the culture of turf cutters, and the bog songs of Irish poets, along with a title—*The Bog-Man's Daughter.*

Here's the beginning of the play to give you a sense of it:

Deidre enters, carrying a basket of turf. She is a young Irish woman, bare-footed in a peasant dress. She takes out a letter and recites:

Deidre:
"I'm nobody. Who are you? Are you nobody too?
How dreary to be somebody. How public like a frog.
To tell your name the live long day to an admiring bog."

That's a poem. By the great American poet Emily Dickinson. Me brother put it in his letter, just to make fun of me. He thinks I'm wasting my life "telling me name the live long day to an admiring bog." "Why don't you come to America?" he writes. "Be a factory girl in the great cotton mills of Lowell, Massachusetts," he says. "Wake up, sister! This is the 19th century!"

(she crumples up the letter)

Well, he can take his 19th century and stick it! Along with his cotton mills. I say, I was born and raised here by the bogs, and by God I'll die here too. Just like me father before me. They called him, "Fear na Mona," the Bog Man. He could cut more clods of turf in a day than any man in Connemara.

She picks up slaene and starts *"digging turf."*

This is a *slaene*. It's used to cut peat. This here is peat. It burns cleaner than coal. . . .

You can tell the quality of the peat by squeezing it. If clean water runs off, it's poor. If you get a brown dirty runoff, it's good enough for cooking. But the real rich peat to heat your home, why that squeezes through your fingers like chocolate pudding.

The important thing about this process is that we approached the play from the point of view of both the information and the drama. We asked: what are the neat things about bogs, and how can we tell that story. This is the start of almost every playwriting process in the museum—a dual focus. It was no different, for example, with the rain forest play *The Ballad of Chico Mendes*. In that case we had the drama first—the murder of Mendes—and had to find ways to weave interesting rain-forest information into it (how you tap rubber, what the forest protects, why they burn it down, etc.).

You may say, well, of course, you have to approach the play from both angles—the information and the drama—but this is easier said than done. If you are too respectful of the information you can drown your play in fact glut, and if you leap too quickly to a dramatic form, the show often may seem facile, stagy, and juvenile, like you are putting on a high-school skit.

No, what's called for in most cases is to start looking for the play as if you are daydreaming. Listen to the educators, experts, and exhibit planners respectfully, but not *too* respectfully. Let yourself tune out when they load you up with documents and see what fascinating tidbit brings you back. Do enough research to know the territory but not so much you miss the forest for the trees. Skim the material, sift through it for pleasure, and see what emerges naturally. Chances are the pillars of your play will make themselves known to you without much effort if you just look for what moves you emotionally.

After all, the reason to put on a play—rather than build a model, paint a picture, make a video or CD-ROM—is that plays are done by human beings and human beings are emotional creatures. We laugh, we weep, we rage, we grieve. And if you can move an audience, chances are they will remember the experience (and the information associated with it) much more vividly.

So, at the beginning of every playwriting process, it may be contrary to a good work ethic, but I recommend that

you let your mind wander and follow your heart.[2] But what does it mean, really, on a practical level to "follow your heart"? How do you look for the emotional center of your play? I would like to suggest that you look for it where playwrights have always looked for it: in story, in character, in setting. With *The Ballad of Chico Mendes*, you have all three—Rubber Tapper Murdered in Rain Forest. But for many museum plays, it is not so obvious.

It was not at all clear, for instance, what the heart of the play should be for the joint project of the Museum of Science and WGBH-TV, the local public television station. The WGBH staff wanted the play to tie in with their series, *A Science Odyssey*, on the science and technology achievements of the 20th century. It wasn't that there were no good stories (The Manhattan Project, for instance) or no interesting characters (Einstein, Freud) or no evocative settings (the Wright brothers' bicycle shop); in fact, there were too many good things and nothing to hold them together. So, after skimming through tomes of discoveries and inventions, breakthroughs and innovations, and a number of discussions with Mike Alexander, I remembered a story about a woman I had met who had received a heart transplant. This heart transplant had set her on an emotional roller coaster which turned her life upside down. And when we considered all the science and technology that had to have been put in place for this modern miracle to happen, it seemed a natural for focusing the material and giving it, well, heart-felt passion.

Here are some passages from the play to show how we worked the theme into the rhythms of the language:

(Rosie, a young woman with a bad heart, is pacing in her room waiting for her beeper to ring.)

Rosie:
My mother had a bad heart, and my grandmother before her, and I had a bad heart and I was waiting to die. Actually, I was waiting for my beeper to ring. Cause those were my two choices. Either my beeper would ring or I would die. My mother never had this choice, nor her mother before her. They didn't even have beepers.

(Pause)

Lucky me. Without the beeper, this story would not have happened.

(Joey appears. A young man with a strong heart, preparing to take off in a hang glider.)

Joey:

I look out over the cliff. I check the wind. I check my rig. I ask myself one more time: why am I throwing myself off a 50-foot cliff?

(He leaps.)

Get the Polaroid, Ma! Look out below!!!!

(He gets up on a table in the image of flying.)

Rosie:
(to the audience)
The hang glider . . .

Joey:
Higher and higher . . .

Rosie:
—without the hang glider . . .

Joey:
Higher and higher. . .

Rosie:
—this story would not have happened.

Joey:
Up! Up! Up! Really soaring now!

Rosie:
This is a purely 20th-century story.

Joey:
Ludwig von Beethoven, Isaac Newton, Alexander the Great never did this!

Rosie:
And I am a purely 20th-century phenomenon.

Joey:
This is life, this is life, this is . . .

(He freezes. Sound of a crash.)

Rosie:
Omigod! Omigod! The next thing I know there's an ambulance at my door. And I'm signing my will and packing my toothbrush.

Joey:
(As if watching himself from a great distance.)
And 200 miles away a helicopter lifts off with a heart packed in a picnic cooler.

Rosie:
Thank goodness for the combustion engine.

Joey:
The rotary propeller.

Rosie:
The superhighway.

Joey:
The radar screen.

Rosie:
The picnic cooler.

What makes this play work is the audience's strong identification with the character, also the fast-paced narrative that sweeps the audience along emotionally. In the course of this piece, Rosie will receive a new heart, fall in love, get married, lose her husband, and have a baby. Like the 20th century itself, her life will appear to be a wild ride through incredible circumstances. Done badly this is mere melodrama. Done well, this is good theater.

But, as I've said, not every picture tells a story and not every exhibit has a built-in drama. So, if the subject matter doesn't easily suggest a good story, or central character, or a world to explore, you have to find substitutes for these more traditional forms of glue: a kind of collage effect. By "collage" I mean a drama that constantly shifts style while dancing around a central idea or theme, sort of like a variety show.

The Leonardo da Vinci play was constructed in just this manner. It seemed inappropriate to have someone play Leonardo as an old man, since we don't really know what he thought, said, or felt. It also seemed boring to try to make a drama out of Leonardo's last struggling days since these held few moments of action or conflict that would be more than of passing interest. Instead, the collage form suggested itself immediately since this was the form of his famous notebooks. And one of our objectives was "to see as he saw," highlighting his observational skills.

So to create this piece, we started making lists of all of our favorite Leonardo things. Pretty quickly the list looked something like this:

> *Leonardo's obsession with the Deluge*
> *His dissection of cadavers*
> *The Mona Lisa*
> *Investigation of light*
> *Leo, the impresario, writing jokes in his notebooks*
> *The earth as a macrocosm, man as the microcosm*
> *Why sea-shells are found on mountain tops*
> *Etceteras.*

What finally came out of all this was a show that constantly shifted mood and style—horror for the dissection, lyricism for the *Mona Lisa*—a different "mask" for each of the faces of Leonardo da Vinci. Here is just one "mask" from *The Masque of Leonardo da Vinci*—a passage from Leonard's notebooks imagining the Deluge, edited to make the audience experience the terror and power of the artist's apocalyptic vision.

Mask Maker:
Darkness . . . wind . . . tempests at sea . . .

Actor:
Darkness, wind, tempests at sea, floods of water, forests on fire, rain, earthquakes, bolts from heaven, mountains in ruin, devastation of cities.

Mask Maker:
Whirlwinds, water spouts. . .

Actor:
—ships broken to pieces, beaten on rocks. Hail stones, thunderbolts.

And lightning—

Mask Maker:
—lightning!

Actor:
—lightning from the clouds illuminating everything.

Mask Maker:
This is the apocalypse! His vision of the end of time!

Actor:
On the hilltops terrified animals collect together in a frightened crowd.

Mask Maker:
Desperate men, weapons in hand, defend small shelters against beasts of prey.

Actor:
In the waters, children cling to capsized boats as the tempest sweeps more victims from the shore and rolls the waters over the bloated bodies of the drowned.

Mask Maker:
Ah, what dreadful noises rend the air.

Actor:
Ah, how many mothers weep over their drowned sons and shake their fists at heaven to curse the wrathful gods.

Mask Maker:
Ah, how many fathers in anguish, gnaw the knuckles of their own clasped hands till the raw flesh bleeds.

Actor:
The crazed ones take their own lives, flinging themselves from lofty cliffs, falling on their own weapons.

Mask Maker:
—while others fall upon their knees in silent prayer. . .

Actor:
—and cover their eyes that they might not see. . .

Mask Maker and Actor:
. . . the cruel slaughter of the human race by the wrath of God.

(Whispering, as the lights go down, simultaneously)

Darkness, wind, tempests at sea, bolts from heaven, mountains in ruin, devastation of cities.

And lightning from the clouds illuminating everything.

All dramatic writing is a form of music, with rhythms and sounds, the sensuality of language, carrying the burden of the passions. And, as all performers know, words are often the most powerful "actions" on stage. So, even in the absence of plot or character or setting, theater can convey a feeling tone by the very shape of the words. Of course, all plays must have coherence. And some plays should be written using classical forms. But, often, by freeing yourself from a rigid stylistic approach into which everything must be jammed you can allow the content to dictate the form, much as the songs in a musical cabaret shift with the changing moods of the cabaret singer.

And, of course, it is essential to keep in mind all the theatrical devices that have enlivened theater through the ages: music, dance, mask work, puppetry, and, most of all, the outrageous silliness of clown work. Our play about the Titanic disaster was narrated by an actor dressed as a crab with oven-mitts for claws. The Mars rock digger for our play about the Russian space program was a pooper-scooper. Our play about the science of sexuality was performed by aliens from another planet that had determined the dominant life form on earth must be the automobile.

Laughter: there's nothing like it to get them on your side.

But it needn't be constant laughter. Of all the stylistic devices in the variety- show format, the most effective I have found is a modulation between comedy, fascinating information, and passionate emotions. Thus, the Titanic play begins with the crab comically introducing herself as a starlet in the Titanic movie, moves on to describe the self-assured technology that made the ship supposedly unsinkable, solemnly stops to consider what the owner of the White Star Line must have felt as he slipped into a half-empty lifeboat, and ends in a philosophical mood, considering the myth of Daedelus, the archetype of technological arrogance.

Of course, let me repeat: if you've got a good story, just tell a good story. If you've got fascinating characters, just let them speak. No need for "the variety-show format" if more traditional and straightforward forms work. Still, nine times out of ten the necessity of getting certain key information across will require a kind of protean approach to playmaking that allows you to shift tone, voice, style, and mood whenever the content demands it.

This only works, though, if the audience is prepared for it. Prepared for something different. Prepared for an unpredictable show. It is essential, then, that from the very beginning you convince them that the performance will not be like television sitcoms or the downtown plays they are used to. But more like a minstrel show, a traveling circus, a street performance.

To pull this off, you have to make it seem like the presentation is informal, rough, maybe even something thrown together. The play about the Russian space program used toys and tin cans to represent rockets as if the museum couldn't afford real models. Another play, about sunken ships, used office chairs on wheels to represent the boats. The play called Stuck in Time (about the LeBrea tar pits) began with the actor wandering through the audience asking if anyone had the time. And the date. And the year. And a play called To the Limit outside the Omni theater was set up to look like a dialogue between an usher and a customer waiting in line.

These tricks of informality allow the audience to relax and enjoy the show without the baggage of expectation. If you are expecting Hamlet you are going to be disappointed. If you are expecting a carny show you can be pleasantly surprised at how moving and enlightening the performance can be. Curiously, the informal style makes great demands on the professionalism of the actors because the work must appear rough and effortless, while hitting its marks emotionally, rhythmically, intellectually.

But of all the techniques for reaching an audience, delivering information, and touching their hearts, the best and most important is the direct narrative voice. In the script samples presented above you will notice that in all of them the actors speak directly to the audience. There is no "fourth" wall, no pretense of dramatic realism. The actors acknowledge that they are telling a story, talking person-to-person.

There is nothing new in this. Shakespeare does this. Brecht does this. Disney does this in *The Lion King*. But while this is only a stylistic option in most professional theatrical situations, in most museum theaters I think it is obligatory. The intimacy of the space, the need to humanize the material, and the necessity of getting information across requires in most cases the ability to talk directly to the audience and tell them what they need to know when they need to know it.

Take the opening of *The Bone Wars*, about two rival paleontologists who hate each other's guts.

Gabby:
Yeeeeeee! Haaaaaa! Greenhorns, listen up, and I'll tell you a story of the Wild West that'll make your blood run cold.

The Wild West! —where life was a gamble, a gun was the law and even science made up its own rules. Yes, Science, that citadel of honesty and mistress to the Truth—Science in the Wild West, pardner, was not pretty.

(*Confidentially to the audience*)

I reckon any of you moms and dads who've brought your youn'uns here to teach 'em respect for the scientific method might just want to saddle 'em up right now. Cause the scientists I'm gonna tell you about—Othniel Charles Marsh and Edward Drinker Cope—were greedier than the golddiggers of '49, meaner than the gunslingers at OK Corral.

This technique involves the audience in a very immediate way. It sucks them into the story and makes them part of the performance. Along the way, it can even draw them into a debate over issues. This was particularly important to us in creating *Mapping the Soul*, a play about the human genome project. Much of this play is realistic "fourth-wall" drama about a woman with a hereditary form of blindness. At crucial moments, though, the woman and her husband interrupt the story to put critical questions to the audience.

Gus:
By 2005, maybe sooner, you will get a printout on a computer, a printout of your genome: where your genes are on each chromosome. This is not science fiction. The army is already developing the equivalent of a genetic dog tag, so that, if a GI gets blown up or something and all that's left is, say, some skin—they can identify the body by his DNA.

Charlotte:
But of course that DNA says a lot more than just who you are. It tells the most intimate information about your inheritance. Your family's tendency perhaps towards Alzheimer's disease, cancer, or heart disease. Some even think there's a genetic tendency toward homosexuality, toward alcoholism. So, who would you want to have such information? Your insurance company? The F.B.I.? The I.R.S.? The junk-mail advertisers?

Talking out to the audience: It moves the story along and tells the audience what they need to know.

Finally, though, the success or failure of a museum theater piece relies less on the techniques, the style, the tricks of the trade, than in the process that is used to create it, a process that must be, from start to finish, a collaboration. Every theater piece, of course, is a collaboration. The writer draws the blueprints, the director supervises the construction, and the actors put the parts in place. But some theater companies, and all theater troupes working in museums, go beyond this and collaborate at every stage in a more intimate fashion.

Certainly, there has to be a close collaboration between the exhibit design team and the theater people to make sure the proper balance is struck between the artistic and educational needs of the project. This is best done by including as many people as possible in the initial brainstorming sessions. The exhibit design team is often a good resource for determining what is emotionally hot and the theater people are often a good sounding board for what is intellectually fascinating.

But, beyond this, it is very healthy to have close collaboration among actors, playwrights, and directors. Many writers forget that a script is not a play, it is only a blueprint. Actors, especially actors that are good at improvisation, can breathe life into a script, determine when the language is too convoluted or banal, discover actions that speak louder than words, and investigate the emotional underpinnings of the relationships. It is the director's job to supervise this collaboration. It cannot be art by committee. Rather, the director establishes a plan of rotating leadership whereby rehearsals are geared first to serve the writer, then to serve the director, and finally to serve the actors, all the while giving space for feedback from other artists and the educational planners. Collaboration is an art in itself—it take time, patience, modesty, and good will—and must be studied and practiced to succeed. [3]

The opening of *The Ballad of Chico Mendes* is a good example of what I consider a good collaboration. I'll close with that. The play begins with a song that was created in collaboration with a composer. The actors, a man and a woman, both improvised and developed the role of Chico (giving us, often, two Chicos on-stage). Their opening dialogue was created in collaboration with a choreographer who set the language to a tango. And the clapping of the hands, which suggests scene changes and gunshots, is a directorial device developed in rehearsal. Most important-ly, the opening gets across the major message the exhibit designers wanted us to stress: understanding, love, and respect for the Amazon, which we encapsulated in the exultant chorus "Viva Amazonia."

Chico Man & Chico Woman:
(singing)
This is the story of Chico Mendes,
And the victorious movement he led,
Like the rubber tree standing tall,
He bled for us all.

Fires were burning the trees to the ground,
Chain saws were cutting the canopy down,
Then they tried to take his land,
He took his stand.

Viva Amazonia! Viva Amazonia! Viva Amazonia!

Long life to life. . . long life to life in the Amazon.
Long life to life. . . long life to life in the Amazon.

Here comes the ballad of Chico Mendes,
Battered with violence, riddled with lead,
If you choose to take his lead,
You, too, may bleed.

Yes, like the rubber tree,
Your heart, too, may bleed.

(Both actors clap hands.)

Chico Woman:
Listen: Chico learns he is going to die.

Chico Man:
Can you imagine what it's like to know you are going to die?

(Walking around each other like flamenco dancers, intimate, wary, and dangerous.)

Chico Woman:
You're not sick, you're not weak, and yet. . .

Chico Man:
And yet. . . Someone comes up to you—

Chico Woman:
A friend, perhaps. . .

Chico Man:
—and the friend was talking to another friend. . .

Chico Woman:
—who was talking to a stranger, and the stranger said:

Chico Man:
Tell Chico Mendes he is going to die.

(Pause)

Both:
(overlapping)
They are going to kill me.

(They clasp one another in an intimate, deadly embrace, and dance a tango.)

Chico Woman:
That's how it is in the rain forest where I live.

Chico Man:
They give you an *anuncio*, an announcement of your mur-der before they kill you.

Chico Woman:
They scare you. . .

Chico Man:
They torture you. . .

Chico Woman:
To make you see death in every stranger's look. . .

Chico Man:
—grief in every friend's face.

Chico Woman:
It's as if you are already dead.

Chico Man:
A ghost, with no future.

Chico Woman:
No hope.

Chico Man:
So you live in the present.

Chico Woman:
You hug the present.

Chico Man:
Smother with affection each second of each day.

Both:
What good is a corpse,
What good is a corpse,
I Chico Mendes want to live!
I want to live!
(They clap hands. End of scene.)

Eleventh Commandment of museum theater: thou shalt leave them with something to think about.

Notes

1. (Here I'm restricting myself to work I've done in the Boston Museum of Science, but it is the same all over: the Boy Scout Museum in Kentucky wants something on the founders of the Boy Scouts; the Labor Museum in Lowell wants to tell the story of the strike of 1912, etc. etc.)

2. The poet Denise Levertov, following the lead of Gerard Manley Hopkins, has an excellent essay on "Organic Form" in which she advises writers to search for form as if it were already there only shrouded in mist. The mists can be dispersed by searching for the "inscape" of things, the inner landscape that makes disparate things cohere. And you find the "inscape" by examining in yourself the "instress," the inner emotions that the subject matter evokes.

3. Improvisation is a waste of time, but a creative waste of time. Collaboration is inefficient, but a creative kind of inefficiency. For artists who have not worked this way, my main suggestion is to get the actors together after the first draft and start working with them in the presence of the writer from this point on. Invite the education staff to review the first draft before rehearsals start, but don't invite them to watch the actors until the second draft is written. Let the writer create a script that is too long; it is easier to cut than to add. And choose a director who enjoys creating a team because it is the director's job to handle the interpersonal relations which must be cooperative if the collaboration is to succeed.

RESPONSE TO *Playwriting for Museums*

ROBERT A. RICHTER

The 11 commandments of museum theater according to Jon Lipsky (1–9: "Thou shalt not be boring"; 10: "Thou shalt always deliver the information" and 11: "Thou shalt leave them with something to think about") are excellent guiding principles in the development of museum theater scripts. In many respects the development of museum theater scripts is no different than the development of scripts for other venues. A playwright should never bore the audience and the play should stimulate the audience either emotionally or intellectually no matter what venue. The main distinction between museum theater and non-museum theater is the importance of the delivery of information or content. The potential for boring the audience comes into play with the drive, within the museum context, to deliver the information and be educational. The challenge in museum theater is to entertain the audience while educating them. The successful script is the one where the audience is not directly aware of the educational content and the learning process.

Lipsky raises other key points about museum theater that should not be forgotten and in some cases should be explored in greater detail. He mentions the length of plays, the similarities to street theater, the importance of involving the audience, the collaborative nature of theater, and the intimacy and nontraditional nature of the performance spaces.

Museum theater can be compared to street theater. Generally the museum patron is not visiting the museum to see theater. If the visitor is even aware that a particular museum has a theater program, the viewing of theater will only be part of the visitor's experience. The theater piece is part of a much larger environment with other activities designed to attract the visitor's attention. Museum visitors can be compared to window shoppers. They are a transient audience, on the move; but sometimes they take a moment here or there to pause because their attention has been drawn to something of interest. Although visitors will stop to explore something, they rarely linger in one spot to await the start of a program. This means that the audience for a theater piece are those individuals who are in the vicinity when the piece begins. As a result museum theater should take its cue from street theater. The script needs to quickly hook the audience. As the audience is being reeled in they should be engaged, entertained, and educated and then released to experience other aspects of the museum. When commissioning plays I have instructed and pushed playwrights to write 15-minute scripts, which can be a difficult task. Invariably the final product is about 20 minutes in length, which is perfect. Brevity is key. There is no time for long exposition and every word must count.

The playwright for museum theater must also consider the space or environment in which the play will be performed. Some museums have theaters with varying degrees of technical support, ranging from none to some. But, many museums do not have theaters, or they specifically choose to present performances in galleries, recreated environments, or outdoors. There are many questions the playwright needs to ask. Is there a defined playing area? Who is the audience (children, teens, adults, families)? What is the expected audience size? Will there be seats for the audience? There are many more logistical questions that can guide the playwright. Again, this is an area where museum theater differs from more traditional theater venues. A playwright would not normally need to know the answers to these questions. Whereas, in devel-

oping museum theater scripts the playwright has to create a piece that fits the environment, in both a physical and programmatic sense.

The most successful museum theater pieces are those that involve the audience. Participation on the part of the audience helps to engage them and can solidify the educational message. But it is important that the audience be treated with the utmost respect when it comes to participation. The audience must succeed in their participation. It is the playwright's responsibility to create ways for the audience to participate that are simple, challenging, and voluntary. A playwright should avoid asking questions that are too obvious. For example, scripting that an actor ask the audience what he is holding when it is something as obvious as an umbrella. Many playwrights (and teachers for that matter) resort to this type of participation. The answer to the question is so obvious that in many cases it does not elicit a response. The audience perceives it as a trick question and is reticent to answer, because they are afraid of being put in a situation that will make them appear foolish. These types of questions can be demeaning to the audience. A more successful form of participation is one that assigns a role to the audience or an audience member and puts them in a position to contribute to the action of the play. The participation can either be physical or vocal, but it must advance the story.

Theater is a wonderful technique to help the museum audience gain a frame of reference or perspective on other programs and exhibitions. As a result, script development and eventual production must be collaborations. Lipsky mentioned that the collaborative process in the museum theater context must go beyond the theater practitioners and include exhibition designers, museum educators, and content specialists. The ideal situation is when a theater piece is being developed along with the exhibition and all the parties can work together in developing a cohesive visitor experience. But, in many instances the theater piece is developed after the exhibition. The purpose for creating a play might be to reinvigorate long-term exhibitions or to employ a different technique making the exhibition accessible to a broader audience. Under these circumstances the playwright does not have the benefit of a true collaboration. In any event, the approach should still be collaborative, in that the playwright must consider all that has come before and create a script that fits into the existing context.

The most important thing to consider in the development of a script, as with any museum program, is to keep the audience central in the experience. The idea of putting the visitor at the center of the museum experience is what has driven many museums to use theater as an interpretive technique. Theater enables the museum to strike a direct relationship with the audience by bringing the human element into the interpretation of science, art, and history.

CHAPTER 3

USE OF IMPROVISATION IN MUSEUM THEATER

Sheli Beck, Executive Director
Victorian Living History Museum, The Astors' Beechwood Mansion, Newport, Rhode Island

Dear Diary,
Today I auditioned for the greatest job. It's for a Victorian Living History Museum in Newport, Rhode Island, called The Astors' Beechwood Mansion. They are hiring actors to portray Victorian characters from history as both Aristocrats and Domestics. The job is called an interpreter/guide. It sounds like a great job because all the tours are improvised. It is like impromptu speaking—no scripts but with a focus for each of the rooms of the museum. It's in a mansion—and I will get to live there if I get the job. For the audition I had to perform a monologue, sing, and waltz. They have a great vintage dance program. I also had to perform in a few improvisation games. In one scene I was pretending to be a domestic being scolded for breaking a china teacup. I'll keep my fingers crossed. . . .

Museum-theater improvisation is the tool interpreter/guides at the Astors' Beechwood Mansion use to create a more memorable and entertaining experience than a traditional historic-house tour. At the Beechwood Mansion we believe that the use of improvisation by an actor wearing period costumes in a first person interpretation enhances the visitor's guided tour experience by creating a visual stimulation that is retained more prominently in their memory. This technique is well established at The Astors' Beechwood Mansion.

In 1981, this Victorian Living History Museum was first called a "Theatrical Tour" that used actors performing improvisationally as witty characters in colorful period garments. The concept was a style of tour that was a fun flashback to a time gone by. Actors used humor for every fact that was shared practically on a one-to-one humor to fact ratio. As the theater program progressed, we developed an environmental style of improvisation, with specific characters in each room of the museum, such as a cook in the kitchen, a debutante having an etiquette lesson in a receiving room, and dancers in the ballroom. Due to budget cuts, this style, though very educational, was

unable to be continued. Today, 17 years later, the museum theater program is more focused on historical accuracy of the Victorian characters and their daily lives, rituals, and routines. The concept of the guided tour is to have actors as interpreter/guides portraying characters of their age range in an improvised tour of the mansion. It is still a fun flashback to a time gone by, but the humor-to-fact ratio is more realistic of a family member showing family friends their home. The humor comes from the honesty of the differences of yesterday and today.

The one theme of the museum that remains constant is the use of improvisation. The current staff of interpreter/guides portrays characters that are age-specific, that of the actors themselves. Each develops two characters: a nonfictional aristocrat character who is fully researched and a fictional domestic (or servant) character created from historical information from the period on the duties of domestics. The museum tour, set in the year 1891, gives visitors the experience of stepping back in time to "call" on the Astor family. Mrs. Astor was known as the "Queen of American Society," the creator of the first American social register and the home's owner in 1891. She is also the mother of John Jacob Astor IV, who was the richest passenger to die on the *Titanic*. The Astor fortune was originally made through fur trading and real estate by John Jacob Astor I, a German immigrant who became the richest man in America—the great American dream realized! His story is excellent material for creating fascinating tales of a time gone by for today's visitors.

Visitors to the Victorian Living History Museum meet at least three different characters of different classes. The guided tour is 45 minutes in length and begins with an orientation presented by a domestic who explains the tour concept and the rules of the facility. There is a staff of eight interns and five production team members who perform in the museum three to five days a week and participate in the Astor Ball, an evening of 1890s songs and dances held on Tuesday evenings June to October.

Improvisation is the major technique used by the interpreter/guides who create the Victorian environment of the Beechwood Mansion. These staff members are actors who have been selected for their ability to speak articulately and cleverly in an impromptu situation. They also must be able to sing in an opera choral style and participate in vintage dance. These required skills are based on what were commonplace abilities for the 19th-century aristocrat. Beechwood specifically hires professional actors. This level of talent is integral to the success of the interpretation presented to visitors. The ability to train an actor in the history of the period portrayed is much more efficient than training a historian to be an actor. The quality of your museum's interpretation is only as high as the training and skill of your staff. The choice to use improvisation rather than a scripted format should be made according to what best suits your facility. To choose improvisation provides a less structured, free-flowing exchange between character and visitor. However, it requires a significantly large amount of training in order to have well-prepared characters representing your facility.

Dear Diary
I got the job!! I am going to play Mrs. John Jacob Astor IV— Ava. She was considered the most beautiful woman in America in 1891—what an honor! What a challenge to look that good every day. I will also portray a house maid, a fictional role that I will create. Beechwood is sending me information on Ava and on housemaids of the era. I will also get a script, outlining the museum's format. I am to memorize the entire script, which has everything from time limits for each room to details on the collection. I will have a 21 day training period. It sounds intense! They said that learning these roles, as an interpreter/guide, is comparable to learning the role of Hamlet. I am simply thrilled. I am really flattered because they said the casting team sees about 2,000 auditions all over the United States, and they chose me!

The technique of improvisation is often described as the art of acting without the use of a script, to be spontaneous with dialogue within a set of given circumstances. In museum theater the set of circumstances is historical fact, but to most theater performers improvisation is recognized as a technique of comedy. There are "Comedy Sportz" competitions throughout the United States where actors perform improvisation games in a competitive atmosphere. Used in museum theater, the technique of improvisation can give the visitor and the actor a personal experience that fits the needs and expectations of the situation. It is more interactive than scripted material, which can be limiting to visitors who feel they want to know more or different information.

Improvisation can be an excellent tool to bring stories to life that are amusing, touching, or even disturbing. It allows the visitor to question the character and the situation. The conversations that occur from these interactions are some of the best educational opportunities available to all ages. Imagine being able to ask questions of your favorite painter about his work and lifestyle while he is creating his greatest piece. What questions would you ask to gain information on his use of color or texture, or to learn about the painter's eating or sleeping habits? For another example, imagine that while you're visiting an art collection, a wacky security guard shares an opinion that evokes a point of view very different from your own, empowering you to state your opinion and create an exchange.

The goal of this situation for the actor would be to have you, the visitor, defend your opinion, giving you a sense of self-satisfaction. It is the chance for conversation that makes improvisation such a good tool for heightening the visitor experience. The opportunity to chat with John Jacob Astor IV and resist the temptation to warn him about his journey on the Titanic is just one of the interesting moments created with improvisation at Beechwood on a daily basis. The young actress who will portray Mrs. John Jacob Astor IV will train for 21 days of intense lessons, learning the history of the Astor family, the United States in general, and Newport in particular. She will also attend classes on etiquette, fashion, verbiage, conversation, dance, and voice. All of this comprises the regular "finishing school" for the actors who will become interpreter/guides at Beechwood Mansion.

Dear Diary,
Rehearsals began yesterday and I have a lot to learn. I think my characters are so interesting and I can't wait to learn more about Ava. She is often called the New Mrs. Astor because she was married in 1891, the year the museum is set in. I took my first Beechwood Living History tour today, it was a guided format but they say the Astor Ball will be done environmentally.

Improvisation at Beechwood Mansion is done in two different styles: a guided tour format and an environmental format. Both forms require the same amount of training and information sharing; the difference is how each style controls the movement of the visitors.

In the guided tour format our goal at Beechwood Mansion is to have visitors feel as though they have arrived for an "inspection of the cottage." We ask the guests in our orientation to suspend their disbelief and take on the role of a society friend of Mrs. Astor being shown about by someone who knows the home. We give visitors a premise that they, as members of Mrs. Astors' social register, "The 400," have been invited for dinner the next evening. This allows visitors to feel more comfortable when asking or answering questions.

The difficulty of this guided tour is that there is a time limit of three minutes per room, which must be closely observed by the actor. This time limit was determined by the fact that the visitors must move through the facility—there are no chairs for sitting. Without this or a similar structure, the entire flow of the facility would be affected. Although a time restriction may seem limiting for an actor, the guided tour format ensures that guests will receive specific information because the actor has the duty to share certain facts about each room. This format makes it possible to give visitors information while they move from room to room. The goal of the interpreter/guide is to make the experience more like a conversation, encouraging the visitors to interact, asking and answering questions.

This type of improvisation-based guided tour is also an excellent training tool for those learning the material. It gives the actor/interpreter more structure for sharing creative stories. Our script at Beechwood is done room by room with certain facts to be discussed; each room has a theme which makes it easier for the actor to create a "through line" of information by intertwining that information into the stories. For example, the Language of the Calling Card can easily segue into information about 18th century paintings in the receiving room, by using as a through line a discussion of how guests would wait to be received by Mrs. Astor. As the actors are creating their characters and learning the verbiage of the Victorian Era they can work on one room at a time to feel more secure with the character, information, and structure of the guided-tour format.

Dear Diary,
Boy, am I learning an entirely new vocabulary. Today we learned ways to add to the environment of Beechwood by doing "pop-ins." They are fun ways to add life to the mansion and show how little life has changed over a hundred years in areas like sibling rivalry and problems between spouses. Patrick, who is playing my husband Jack, is so fun to interact with. Our pop-ins are so much fun because we (Jack and Ava) have an arranged marriage and don't like each other.

At Beechwood, new interpreter/guide staff members are scheduled as part of training to perform "pop-ins." This is a less-than-one-minute interaction between characters. A pop-in can be done silently. For example, a maid is cleaning a mirror until she notices that guests have entered the room, whereupon she stops cleaning and is excused. The character showing the guests about would then explain, "we should never see the domestics toiling; it might upset our delicate sensibilities." Pop-ins can also be a simple introduction of a sibling who wishes to gain a dance partner for the next ball. There is also an informational pop-in, in which a character arrives to share one of the points to be discussed in the room. This must be planned ahead so that both staff members know what is expected, and information will not be missed or repeated. For example, an informational pop-in might involve guests entering the dining room to find a bachelor sitting at the table practicing his dinner conversation. When the bachelor is discovered, he explains how nervous he is about the upcoming meal because Mrs. Astor's rules for dinner conversation are so strict, and he wants to make a good impression. He will explain the rules to the visitors, who have assumed the premise that they too will be at dinner. He may even ask them to help clarify a few points so he can be more assured. This creates a scene between the actor and the visitor. The goal of the interpreter/guide is to teach the visitors about the rituals of dinner, but the pop-in scene makes it appear as though the visitor is empowering the character and avoiding embarrassment at the fictitious upcoming dinner.

Dear Diary,
Tonight was my first Ball at Beechwood. I was only a spectator, but I was genuinely impressed. The first part of the event

was an environmental tour in which there was a different focus in each room. It was funny to watch Chris as Mr. Chanler teach guests to waltz, and I really enjoyed chatting with Marci, who played Mrs. Wilson, about the art of flirtation and courtship rituals. But the best part was the activity in the ballroom. It seemed so real and the dancing was so beautiful. I truly felt as though I was in 1891. I can't wait to do this myself.

The second style of improvisation used at Beechwood Mansion is called environmental. This style allows visitors to mingle with many characters at their own pace while asking their own questions to engage the characters in conversation. To be most effective in information sharing at Beechwood, we give each room a theme, such as the art of flirtation, life of a debutante, courtship rituals, arranged marriages, or ballroom etiquette. Actors are trained to engage visitors in conversation and begin with introductions as guests enter the room. The environmental style of improvisation gives the attraction a more realistic feeling, as though the historic house were truly lived in. Having servants beating rugs, cooks making soup, debutantes in tutorial, bachelors betting on croquet matches, and matrons lounging in the shade, all add to the creation of the Victorian environment at Beechwood.

An advantage of using improvisation instead of a script is that the conversation is just that—conversation. The visitor's experience, whether guided or environmental, becomes an interaction between two time periods, stepping back to the past. Guests can ask questions and the actors are trained to answer. Actors also engage the visitors by asking yes or no questions, which gives the visitor confidence that they are in a safe environment and that they are not being mocked. This unscripted opportunity gives visitors a chance to ask whatever questions they have always wondered about, including silly topics that can only be addressed in a one-on-one environment, such as questions about hygiene, family relations, or the marriage restrictions of domestics.

At Beechwood from June to October we recreate a small Victorian ball called the Astor Ball, an evening of 1890s songs and dances. Part of the success of this is the environmental style of interaction between actor and visitor. The evolution of this event began in 1991, when it was known as the Thé Dansante. In its early stages this event

had a guided tour, but it was only given by two actors, and the rest of the cast was waiting to dance in the ballroom. In 1994, the name changed to a more understandable title, The Tea Dance Tour. This time the tour was a collection of scripted fourth-wall vignettes in which the visitor was looking in on private moments between characters, much like a scene from a play. As time passed, the abilities of our actors and our collection of vintage dances have grown. We have thus changed the event to focus completely on dance. Along with the recent name change to the Astor Ball and the restructuring to an environmental tour, the ballroom portion of the event has grown to be more interactive with visitors. Attendance has increased with these recent changes, and repeat visitors are very pleased with the current program.

Dear Diary,
Today, rehearsal was tough. The information is frustrating and the time limits are difficult. I just can't seem to keep all the facts straight in my head. These time limits are impossible!!!!! I want to do this well, but sometimes I just feel like a regular tour guide. Maybe I should have done regular summer stock this season. Who knows?

The weaknesses of using improvisation are easily identified. The first and foremost is the very vehicle by which improvisation creates its successes: actors. They must possess a high caliber of talent—and must be well trained. They also must be well monitored. The same creative sense that gives actors the skill to create interesting, witty characters can also give them a sense of having too much creative ability and a tendency to stretch the truth, or worse, to answer questions they don't know with a "creative" answer. It is our policy that if an interpreter/guide cannot answer a question because it would mean being clairvoyant in 1891, that character will direct them to someone at the office who can answer the question.

Actors can be passionate about their work. This is a positive element in that they take ownership of a project and treat it with great care. It can be a negative one if they become possessive or temperamental when receiving notes from the director. A museum director must set boundaries with their interpreter/guides and follow them. The director should create strict policy and procedure for everything from appearance to tardiness and even treatment of costumes. These policies must be enforced and supervised. At Beechwood, actors receive a contract that outlines what is expected of them. It includes a strict fining system for violations of the contract. A major part of the first day of training is a review of this fine system. Actors all over the United States are accustomed to similar fining systems and this is a common procedure for most of the people you might hire. If you are using volunteers, it is just as important to have them adhere to the same set of rules and regulations. This will set a tone of consistency for your facility.

To enforce rules at Beechwood Mansion we have a staff member titled Company Manager. She is a member of the production team as well as an actress. She is the supervisor of the immediate atmosphere of the museum. The morale of the company and the experience of the visitors are all directly addressed by this staff member. It is a position comparable in the theater to the stage manager. She is always listening for successful practices and areas needing improvement. Notes are given individually and, for universal issues and challenges, as a group at our daily morning meetings.

The largest challenge of using improvisation in museum theater is that you must train your actors and then trust in their choices. It is impossible to have a constant monitoring system on their every move and statement. Without the trust of the director and company manager there is also a lack of confidence in the performer. With a lack of confidence they will make poor choices both physically and verbally. For example, many everyday contemporary actions, such as saying "OK" while holding our hands on our hips, are not acceptable in the Victorian world. Actors must be careful to avoid these simple mistakes in order to create a thoroughly convincing character. It is important that the director and company manager have a clear system of checking the performances of the interpreter/guides, a system that can both add confidence in the actor as well as correct inaccuracies of character and information.

Another weakness of using improvisation in your interpretation is that the actor must have an outlet when dealing with the public that can help them escape inappropriate behavior by a visitor. There is always going to be someone who doesn't "want to play" who might even say, "cut the acting and get onto the real tour." Occasionally there are also visitors who don't appreciate personal space and try to touch the actor inappropriately. Our policy is that if someone is unpleasant or seems unhappy with their experience, they are sent to the cashier at the front door for a refund. We offer the same service to those with crying children or with children who misbehave by attempting to crawl on the furniture. This gives the interpreter/guide the knowledge that they do not have to be verbally abused by anyone and gives them a way to appease the unhappy customer.

Dear Diary,
Today was supposed to be my first day of tandem tours as Ava, but I was too sick to perform. Becky, our company manager, said that the most beautiful woman in America can't be giving tours with a runny nose and cough. I guess she is right. I wouldn't make the visitors feel very welcome.

A museum using actors should also have a clearly stated sick policy. There is nothing worse than trying to interact with someone with a drippy nose, a scratchy voice, or a face flushed from tension. Because our staff lives and works together, we have a policy that if you are too sick to perform you must go to the doctor and then have bed rest. Disease can spread easily, so we try to encourage healthy living by offering discounts at the local YMCA and healthcare providers from dentists to chiropractors.

Dear Diary,
Tonight I had such an experience as an actress. As part of training we had a recreation of the Victorian dinner ritual. It was an amazing experience as well as a great meal: nine courses! It was incredible to be totally immersed in my character for three and a half hours. Stanislavsky really was on to something with his acting theories. He would have loved working at Beechwood.

As part of the training process at Beechwood Mansion, we recreate at least three moments from the daily routine of the Victorian era. This is a technique used by Constantin Stanislavsky at the Moscow Art Theater and discussed in his book, An Actor Prepares. His theory is that you need to experience the life of the character and the real life situations in the play as a rehearsal technique for the production. This is what we practice at Beechwood. Stanislavsky's theory called "The Magic If" or "what if" is defined as an actor needing to experience an event that a character has experienced by using their imagination and researching to help give the actor a comparable "memory" of the experience. This "memory" enhances the actor's ability to convey the magnitude and depth of the experience to an audience. For instance, if a Beechwood actor wants to know what it was like to go the beach in 1891, she should look at photos and read first hand accounts of beach experiences. She could also put on a Victorian bathing costume and try to recreate the experience. Following this, the actor can ask herself, "what if" my character were to go to the beach. She can then better relay the experience from a personal point of view and have vivid images to convey to visitors.

We use the "what if" at Beechwood by providing "live-in" experiences for our actors. Our most successful experiences are no longer than three hours and the situations are very active: theme tea parties, morning rituals for domestics, croquette tourneys, and the nine-course family dinner. These experiences are structured as closely as possible to the real life of Victorians, taking into account the modern day and financial limitations. In the past, we would try to recreate an entire "day in the life." It was a marvelous experience for those who were portraying aristocrats. They were waited on all day while they tended to the major activities of the leisure class: eating, polite conversation, and changing their clothing. The frustration for the director with this format was that everyone was unfocused by the time the big event of the day—the nine-course dinner—arrived. Those who were cast as domestics often ended the day in tears from the stress of the labor and working in restrictive clothing. However, it was a truly remarkable experience. Currently, the individual live-in experiences are conducted separately. Every actor who has worked at Beechwood has proclaimed the live-in experiences to be their favorite and most memorable part of their time with the company.

Dear Diary,
Today was my first official day of tours—boy, what a day. I am exhausted— tired from my toes to my hair. Yes, I have tired hair. This job is such a challenge. I thought it would be so easy, but it isn't. The good thing is that this is very rewarding work for an actress. All day I get to be in character, exploring who that character is and interacting with the audience. The guests at the mansion really challenge you and make you

think so hard. My brain is fried. But it was all worth it. One time today, I asked a little boy if he would sign my dance card, and he said "what is that?" It was the best interaction, with me ending up promising to dance with his older brother. Then, later in the day, I had a group of senior citizens - a bus tour - and they were so much fun. I kinda flirted with this one man and he played right along with me. I think I was able to secure an arranged marriage for Barton, my character Ava's brother, with the conversation.

You will have greater success using improvisation if you allow your interpreter/guides to let their characters develop. Every day at Beechwood Mansion we have a morning meeting where we take a moment for everyone to share what is "the latest" with their characters. For example, the character of Ava Willing Astor was pregnant in 1891, but it wasn't announced right away. So at the end of July (she and her husband Jack were wed in February) when the pregnancy is announced, it gives Ava's character more to share with the visitors and perhaps a new outlook for the father-to-be, Jack Astor. To highlight what has happened during the week for the characters in the museum, the Beechwood Production Team publishes a newspaper for the staff only. It is called The Town Topics, which was the tabloid of the Victorian era. Each issue offers insights on the week's developments and introduces new ideas about future events (which are historical events we have researched from the newspaper). Another example used at a different facility is from Disney's MGM studio "streetmosphere show." At MGM the cast has a board in the actors' trailer, on which each character updates the latest developments in their characters, which are based on Hollywood of the 1940s.

Dear Diary,
Today we had another live-in experience. This was based on the life of a domestic, and it was a good experience to learn more about my housemaid character Elizamarie. We had to do all the morning chores of our characters, which was not easy. It was hot and I had to beat all the rugs, sweep the floors, and dust places I didn't know existed. But in the process I learned a lot about what it must have been like to work in a house like the Astors'. I wish I could read a diary of a housemaid from Newport—that would be amazing. But there doesn't seem to be any available in the area. I suppose one reason is that not many of the girls could write.

At Beechwood we are faced with the challenge of representing a class of persons about whom we have little specific information. We have research regarding the daily routines, pay scale, and nationality of those who served Mrs. Astor. With the exception of her butler, Thomas Hade, her personal secretary, Miss Simrock, the gardener, Mr. Boyd, and her calligrapher, Maria DeBril, we have no names of the domestics who served Mrs. Astor. In creating these fictional characters, each actor is given the job description of his status, which is taken directly from a late 19th-century handbook on domestics. The actor also receives a small biography written by the director, which sets the boundaries for the character. This biography includes family, siblings, any great childhood trauma, nationality, how the character got the job with the Astors, how he came to America the first time, and of course, wishes and dreams for the character. Then the actor is required to create three researched items: a time line on the character, a listing of a typical day in the life of the character, and finally a biography. The biography must be written and must answer the questions that are given to them regarding everything from hygiene to their opinion on an important political issue in Newport in 1891. These same three tasks—time line, daily routine, and biography—are also required by each actor for their nonfictional aristocrat characters as well, but those answers are based on research on the specific character, not created solely from the essence of the era.

Dear Diary,
This is a challenging job indeed. We have a busy schedule and the work is hard, but it is very rewarding. Last night at the Astor Ball, a lady told me as she left that she cried when I sang and that this was the best night of their vacation. It is incredible to have such a responsibility. We always have to remember that these visitors expect everything we say to be historical fact. But more than that, we are teachers. This morning, a Girl Scout troop came through the mansion. I felt like I was making a lasting impression on these young ladies, and I hoped it would be a positive one. Perhaps the visit to Beechwood will inspire one of the girls to become politically active, following the example of the Victorian suffragists. Or maybe a fashion designer will be inspired by our costumes, a historian by our interpretation, or possibly an actress for obvi-

ous reasons. Whenever it's hot and there is a haughty tourist, I remember that I have a responsibility to teach, and hopefully I am able to bring out a positive conversation with that tourist and make their day. It makes me feel powerful to see the awe in their eyes and the smiles on their faces.

The Astors' Beechwood Mansion-Victorian Living History Museum is the success it is because of the use of very talented, well-trained actors performing an improvised recreation of the lifestyle of the Victorian era in the year 1891. It is our experience at Beechwood Mansion that the use of improvisation is the number one key to our success. It is the opportunity for visitors to the Newport area to step back in time and learn what it was like to live in the great mansions of our city. The interaction between character and visitor is a learning experience for both actor and tourist alike; without improvisation that level of interaction would not be possible.

RESPONSE TO *Use of Improvisation in Museum Theater*

AMY GROFF, CURATOR OF EDUCATION, DISNEY'S WILD ANIMAL KINGDOM

Improvisation can lead to a more meaningful experience for visitors at museums such as the Victorian Living History Museum in Newport, Rhode Island. However, I believe it has this effect not just due to the visual stimulation as the author notes. Improvisation originates from the same idea as the current philosophy of zoo design in which immersing your visitors and allowing them to interact with and become part of their surroundings can be fun, capture attention in an entertaining way, and also deliver an inspiring message. Improvisation usually involves drawing the audience into what is happening around them and connecting them to a social art form—theater.

Choosing the right actors for an improvisational experience is tantamount to ensuring its success. The live energy manifested in the exchange between an actor and the audience through improvisation removes any barriers to the understanding and enjoyment of the museum experience. Nonetheless, accuracy and caliber of performance are vital. Training and staff experience is the core ingredient to making improvisational interpretation a successful theatrical medium. The spontaneity that is required for improvisation may make finding the right candidates for these positions difficult.

Interaction is the element that makes improvisation work so well in a museum setting. For too long museums have provided extremely passive experiences in which we hope the visitor reads a sign or talks with a docent. By investing in actors delivering an improvisational experience, the museum increases the chances of the visitor learning from the visit by becoming part of the interpretive encounter. Using the entire museum as a stage enhances the immediacy of the visitor's involvement. Moreover, the transformation from a passive spectator to an active participant at whatever level the visitor feels comfortable lends to the success of the improvisational method of theatrics.

The opportunity to engage the visitor in conversation is an important element of improvisation. By avoiding a script, the conversational element takes place in the institution. Conversations are interactive, thus providing a less passive experience for the visitor and relying on a familiar technique that we engage in each and every day in our own lives. However, improvisation is more than just providing a conversational element to a visitor's experience, as the author notes, because a docent or an educator can accomplish this aspect. Improvisation furnishes the opportunity to immerse and entertain museum visitors thus providing an opportunity to escape reality. It is a tool through which an institution can encourage their visitors to become part of the action whether it be roaming a house in the late 1800s or becoming a researcher in the wilds of Africa.

All the methods of improvisation employed at the Beechwood Mansion—guided tours, "pop-ins," and environmental experiences—seem to be effective and achieve a particular level of visitor engagement in what is happening around them. This is an effective use of different improvisational mediums. I would also note that it is important to provide different levels of visitor involvement as seen in the methods used at the Victorian Living History Museum in an improvisation experience to allow visitors the opportunity to decide how involved in the experience they want to be. We must provide a menu of different opportunities that capture the variety of learning styles.

When selecting the improvisational style of interpretation, it is true that there has to be a great deal of monitoring and boundary setting to control what is being said by the actors. It is therefore important to include in the operational structure of a program utilizing improvisation not only a manager that sets the tone, develops and defines the experience, but also some positions to monitor what is being delivered out in the museum. As we all know, managers tend to become overburdened with the day-to-day management of any organization, such as administrative tasks, meetings, and alike. It is important to employ a coordinator who can periodically monitor what is happening with the guests as well as deal with the actors' concerns.

I would agree also that a clear system of assessment (checking on performance) is essential to combat inaccuracies, as the author notes, but also to provide feedback and capture best practices.

I so enjoyed Ms. Beck's description of the "what if" opportunities for the actors. To encourage the actors to research and become an active participant in the development of their character certainly creates more excitement in portraying that character. Allowing the actor's character to evolve provides a fresh and insightful experience for the actor and can only add to the dynamic of the character they are researching .

The success of any improvisational experience will rest on the caliber of actors employed as well as the system that is set up to ensure their success through monitoring and sharing of best practices. Improvisation is an innovative approach to transporting the visitor back in time to become part of a historical experience; it is also a much more engaging and memorable way to immerse the visitor in the time period.

CHAPTER 4

THEATRE AS INTEGRAL FORCE
CIVILIZATION IS ALIVE!

Susan McLeod O'Reilly
Head, Public Programming, Canadian Museum of Civilization

In the field of museum theatre my predecessor, David Parry, had the stature of a lion. Those of us who knew him were warmed by his soft, generous demeanour. Until his untimely death in 1995, David founded and directed the resident theatre company of the Canadian Museum of Civilization (CMC). In preparing to write this work, the spirit of David has been close by as I consulted his handwritten notes and re-read the several articles he published on the CMC theatre programme. We each bring the cumulation of our particular background and experiences to the assignments we undertake. My own professional background lies not in theatre but in museology. Writing this case study has been a rich learning experience for me.

Scripted first-person interpretation by two members of the CMC theatre company in the Victorian parlour of the Museum's Canada Hall. *Photo by: Harry Foster/Steve Darby of Canadian Museum of Civilization*

Theatre has now survived its first decade at the CMC. In the presentation below I offer an overview of this ten-year history along with an analysis of the role of theatre as an educational tool at the CMC.

SETTING THE STAGE

To your health!, toasts Madame Aubry, no-nonsense mistress of the recreated 18th-century inn inside the Canadian Museum of Civilization. The occasion? An intimate wine-tasting event unfolding in this period dwelling situated along an environment 'streetscape' in the museum. Twenty adults have each paid a fee to be 'guests' at Madame Aubry's table where they will pass a golden evening sipping fine French wines and nibbling hors d'oeuvres developed from ancient recipes, all enjoyed in the reconstructed ambiance of a circa 1730 country inn. Their evening will be led by a wine-tasting expert, or *sommelier*, whose scholarly presentation will be punctuated by the colour commentary of Madame Aubry entertaining her guests with bawdy tales of life in the colony of New France under the regime of King Louis XIV. Educational, you ask? Absolutely. The *sommelier's* vast knowledge of wine is augmented by information on the context of wine drinking and leisure during the New France regime researched by the museum historian responsible for that period of Canadian history. These details are summarized in a booklet distributed to participants at the close of the evening along with full particulars on wines tasted and delicacies eaten. Entertaining? That too. The wrap-around theatrical environment of setting, taste, and personality immerses the participants in this early period of Canadian history in a way they will not soon forget. Education made palatable through a judicious blend of entertainment. Life-long learning at its best because it's memorable. The first-person interpretation provided by bilingual actor, Danielle Aubut, is a key ingredient in the success of this seasonal programme, now two years old and boasting a waiting list of would-be 'guests'.

Elsewhere in the museum on another occasion, a group of senior citizens is brought into the Yuletide spirit by a splendidly attired Saint Nicholas (alias actor Denis Blais) who, through finely crafted storytelling aided by special effects, entertains while informing his audience of the origins of the modern-day culture hero named Santa Claus. Pulling 'living-history' artifacts from his cherry-red sac of goodies, he spins a tale about each object in order to build links in the chain of continuity between Christmas traditions today and of yesteryear. His one-man performance over, the group is guided upstairs to the Victorian mansion situated a little farther along the Canada Hall streetscape from Madame Aubry's New France inn. There the group is greeted by actor Mae Beauchamp in the role of Annie the Irish maid, who describes to the group the holiday traditions celebrated by her master and mistress in this typical middle-class household of late 19th-century Ontario. The seniors wind up their afternoon with tea and fruitcake around a Christmas tree. They leave the museum satisfied that they have enjoyed a learning experience and been "royally entertained in the process."

Voilà, a taste of educational programming at the Canadian Museum of Civilization (CMC). No matter the clientele—school children, day camps, adult learners, or seniors—we do our best to integrate a theatrical experience into the programmes we purpose-develop for special audiences. Then there's the informal visit conducted by the casual visitor—they too have opportunities to exchange with our actors either through first-person interpretation offered in various dwellings along the recreated historical street environment known as the Canada Hall, or through the scripted plays staged within some of the temporary exhibitions.

Certainly, museums have come a long way from the days of William Hutton who, in 1784, recorded an account of his trip to the British Museum. Just to gain entry, a would-be visitor had first to pass inspection by a guard stationed at the gate (must not look too shabby), only to be issued a ticket for admission two weeks hence. Once inside the hallowed halls, Hutton's privilege was to be rushed by a 'guide' through a string of rooms crammed full of a disorganized clutter of unlabeled objects collected from the four corners of the globe. Far from gleaning any knowledge about this exotic cornucopia, Hutton's apparent task was to make his own sense of the objects based on the person-

al scholarship he surely possessed, or why would he have requested entry in the first place? To judge from Hutton's outraged reaction, he was not impressed. In his own words, "If I see wonders which I do not understand, they are no wonders to me. . . . I went out much about as wise as I went in . . ." (quoted in Hudson, 1975: 8-9).

Centuries later, museums have evolved from elitist to populist institution. We want our visitors to "understand." Far from limiting access, museums of the late 20th century channel considerable energy into welcoming and encouraging visits by all people. In fact, success is counted in terms of visitation, based on the industry adage that people vote with their feet. The competition inherent in cultural tourism drives our efforts to make our institutions welcoming, both physically and intellectually. We want visitors to feel good about both the dollars they've spent and the precious time they've invested in having an 'experience' within our four walls as opposed to the walls of a competing leisure pursuit. One of the ways to shape this experience is through the incorporation of theatrical dramatization into exhibition presentations.

Museums of history and ethnography are the last refuge of objects. Pulled from active service, christened "artifact," and placed literally on a pedestal, objects find haven in the preserves of museums. Objects are the raison d'etre of museums—the key to a museum's being—and this is not to be forgotten. Equally and increasingly, though, the modern museum is about information. Information derives from, as well as adds to, the object as a valued form of testimony to lives lived both in the past and in other lands. It is this contextualizing information which brings an object to life in the imagination of the museum visitor. How an object was made, why it was made, when and by whom, for whom: all these details help to invoke the presence of humanity, to tell a story.

Fundamentally, museums of history and ethnography are about telling stories. A curator collects objects and researches information related to the cultural and historical context, from which derive the stories, both exposed and reconstructed. Placed on display, how does the object succeed to tell its story? On its own, an object is inherently mute for the average visitor. Witness Hutton's dilemma back in 1784. A pair of moccasins under glass: beautiful to behold. Beyond the superficial qualities of appearance, which of course bear serious merit, what else do we know about those moccasins: about the people who made them, where and when, how and for what reason, as well as what adventures took place to the person wearing them? To know that information is to invoke a people living in space and time with wondrous and interesting things to say. Lives lived: the essence of the museum experience. Our challenge, for those of us involved in the craft of creating the museum experience, is to invoke those lives. What our modern-day audience seeks is stories.

Scripted first-person interpretation by two members of the CMC theatre company in the Ancien Régime tavern of the Museum's Canada Hall. *Photo by: Harry Foster/Steve Darby of Canadian Museum of Civilization*

Mostly, these stories are told through exhibitions. Now, for those museums who can afford it, a new ingredient has been thrown into the mix: live interpretation, whereby the museum visitor is put into direct contact with a living member of the community treated in a given exhibition. This community may be defined culturally (for example, First Peoples) or according to a certain craft (for example, quilt makers). Contact may take place through performances of music and dance, through hands-on demonstrations, or simply through verbal interactions. Live interpretation is incorporated into exhibitions as the means to illustrate the dynamic element of culture and of art, to show that a community is far from dead, and to build a bridge between artifact and viewer. Theatre is simply that form of live interpretation where an actor assumes the role of a character treated either directly or indirectly in the exhibition.

ENTER THE CHARACTERS

Interpretive theatre has been an institution at the CMC since the magnificent new building opened in 1989. A million-and-a-half people will make the pilgrimage to Canada's national museum of history and ethnography this year to admire the monumental design statement by Metis architect Douglas Cardinal; to take in the countless square feet of exhibitions that includes a children's space, a national postal museum, and the recreated architectural environment of the Canada Hall; to view larger-than-life films in the Imax theatre; and to participate in the slate of interpretive programming designed to showcase the dynamic element of culture. We are Canada's largest and most visited museum.

During the museum planning process in the 1980s, there was a pervasive and consuming will not simply to adopt the latest innovations in museological practice but to be innovators ourselves, to lead the way for others. No longer was it considered acceptable to mount artifacts on display supplemented with explanatory text, graphics, and the occasional diorama. Full contextualization of artifacts favouring maximum intellectual access and using state-of-the-art technology was the modus operandi. The director, George MacDonald, wrote a vision statement, then expanded upon his ideas in the book, A Museum for the Global Village (1989). Expectations were set very high. Ours was to be cutting-edge, a museum for the 21st century. Education made palatable through the injection of a healthy dose of entertainment. The museum experience that draws in visitors, each paying a healthy admission fee to add to the coffers to offset operational expenses government allocations no longer fully cover.

To quote MacDonald:
"Museums must win the opportunity to educate by first entertaining, that is, capturing the imagination of the public. . . . CMC recognizes that enjoyment stimulates learning, and is in itself a worthy goal that does not necessarily require museums to relax high standards; excellence and popularity are mutually achievable. This enables CMC . . . to attract new audiences by emphasizing the entertaining and often participatory qualities of some programmes. Using the theatres and other performance spaces built into the museum, these programmes should bring new visitors and encourage repeat visits, . . . ensuring that there is always something new to see or do. In this way CMC

will respond to people's needs for entertaining and for socializing opportunities (1989:174)."

MacDonald expresses his admiration for the medium of live interpretation:
"By animating the cultural past—or, for that matter, the cultural present—museums can heighten public awareness of heritage and heritage issues, can breathe life into oral traditions, legends, and belief systems, and represent the vitality of a culture. . . (1989:178)."

In 1988 the director of the CMC hired theatre expert, David Parry, to plan and implement a strategy for interpretive theatre at the museum. David's background in theatre of the Middle Ages and Renaissance—which took the form of instructional, popular pieces in an intimate environment—qualified him well for the undertaking. What he lacked in museological background he quickly assimilated through on-the-spot observation and study.

Following a six-month period of reflection, research, and consultation, David released a vision statement for the theatre company in an unpublished document titled *Live Interpretation at the Canadian Museum of Civilization: A Policy Proposal* (1988). The objectives of the Company were set forth, summarized as follows:

- To present first-class theatrical interpretation within the museum in order to contextualize objects and information intellectually, emotionally, socially, and politically.

- To stimulate emotional and intellectual interest in and response to the museum's collections and exhibits.

- To provoke argument, laughter, and tears; to pose questions; to excite.

- To show that the interpretation of history and culture depends partly upon whose perspective you choose in the story you are telling.

- To show that an artifact may have many meanings.

- To reveal the 'other' in ourselves, by showing the familiar in unfamiliar ways and the unfamiliar in our own backyard.

- To demonstrate and embody the idea that the experience the museum offers is immensely enjoyable, stimulating and fun—never ordinary. (: 26)

David set about hiring a complement of actor-interpreters and a stage manager, and began commissioning scripts by professional playwrights. By the time the museum opened in 1989, the company was up and running with an impressive repertoire of scripted plays. The subject matter and the range of performance styles of these pieces was as diverse as the exhibition locations used: women's history and family histories embodied in a vignette on quilt-making; realism and masked ceremonial combined in a piece dealing with current conflicts and re-emerging spirituality in the native community; shadow puppetry telling the Inuit story of Kiviuq the great hunter; a pioneer woman shaping her own vision of the future while her husband works through the winter in a logging camp; King Herod the Great arguing with a museum tour guide about the way history has portrayed him; a railway mail clerk sorting letters as he describes life in the heyday of the Canadian railway mail service; early Jewish immigrants portraying the events and traumatic journeys that brought them to Canada from the Old Country; Haida tales of how Raven brought light into the world and lost his beak; a Basque whaler reliving the whale-hunt in which he nearly lost his leg; and many more. (See Parry, 1994:2.) From simple monologues to complex five-hand plays, the presence of theatre was everywhere evident in the exhibition halls. The company's pace of production was grueling, but wildly exciting and always stimulating. Theatre was well on its way to becoming a firmament of the public programming culture of CMC.

When the company was still in its infancy, anthropologist and museum critic, Jeanne Cannizzo, took an interest in its achievements and praised the vision of "Canada's only professional museum [theatre] company" to:
". . . be about surprise and provocation, with the further objective that it stimulate questions in the visitor: questions about the artefacts, the exhibit, the visitor's own attitudes, and particularly about the nature of the museum experience itself (1994: 45)."

Cannizzo observed that,
". . . the medium of museum theatre when creatively used offers the potential for simultaneously incorporating, acknowledging and criticizing historical attitudes which we may now find culturally offensive. Having done so, it can often proceed to assist visitors in getting much closer to sensibilities radically different from their own (1994: 51)."

Cannizzo had accurately deduced David's vision to make museum theatre do more than animate past lives. He had revealed this motive in one of the objectives (summarized above) where he states that one task of theatre is to show that the interpretation of history depends upon the point of view taken. Himself an academic, clearly David brought a critical stance to the phenomenon of theatre within a museum context. Not only was he intellectually intrigued by the concept of theatre as an interpretive tool within exhibitions, he went a step further to question the very nature of interpretation that is inherent and inevitable in any museum exhibition. From this sprang a desire to bring the public into the fold, to encourage them to reflect critically on what they saw in an exhibition and on how it was presented. A motivating force behind this desire was the ethnocultural subject matter treated by the CMC and its mandate to "promote inter-cultural understanding". In the *Policy Proposal for Live Interpretation at the CMC* (October 1988), David says: "We recognize that there are certain critical issues which . . . come very much to the fore as a programme of live interpretation is developed. These have to do with the Museum's strongly multicultural mandate and the questions of *how* the interpretation of different ethnic Canadian cultures is arrived at, *whose* interpretation it is, and *who* is actually doing the interpreting in the live situation (:16)."

David was careful to work within the context of the exhibition development process, linking his efforts with those of curatorial and educational staff in order to ensure scientific veracity and a thematic linking with the exhibition story line. However, as it was usually he who approached the exhibition team with an idea for a production, by the time David learned about the project it was more often than not too far advanced in production to accommodate a theatre set. Consequently, the actors were obliged to squeeze the performance into the exhibition space as best they could, giving a bit of a tacked-on appearance which was, in fact, the case. One notable exception was the major exhibition, *On Track: The Railway Mail Service in Canada* (1991). From the outset, the designer, curator, and educator agreed upon the need both of hands-on activities and of live interpretation in the show, with the result that a theatre set was physically integrated into the design and actors performed on a regular basis. The public loved it. Given that the curatorial underpinnings of the show were based to large extent on oral history, it only

made sense to animate some of this rich narrative. The scripted story-telling performance augmented the information presented through artifacts, images, text, and decor, by dramatizing the human dimension.

First-person interpretation of the Canadian square timber trade of the 19th century by member of CMC theatre company in the timber shanty of the Museum's Canada Hall. *Photo by: Harry Foster/Steve Darby of Canadian Museum of Civilization*

As we all know, different people learn in different ways. The task of museum educators is to turn this axiom into action. Within the context of exhibition development, that means working with the team first to verbalize the key messages (primary and secondary) to be transmitted by the show and then to identify the appropriate medium for communicating each of those messages. In the case of primary messages—those which the team wants the public absolutely to take away with them—the tact is to repeat and reinforce the messages through an assortment of interpretive media. Such was the process involved in the *On Track* show. I was the curator. Our objective was to find an effective way to share with the public the wealth of stories gleaned from interviews with former railway mail clerks in order to convey one of our primary messages: that the railway mail service was run by people, not machines, who lived aboard trains and were dedicated to "getting the mail through." A few of the stories we reproduced in printed text panels and a take-away gallery guide; several more were presented through film footage shot during the oral-history interviews; and still others we told through the commissioned theatre piece. By conveying the stories through a host of different media, we felt certain to reach all members of our publics through their various learning-style preferences. Theatre was by then a 'happening' thing at the museum, so of course we wanted to involve the company. Our educator entered into a collaborative working relationship with David and the theatre troupe that resulted in a 20-minute monologue performed alternately in English and in French several times daily inside the reconstructed railway mail car forming the heart of the 5,000 square foot exhibition.

During the planning process for the *On Track* exhibition back in 1991, we had hatched another idea for live interpretation, which was to station former railway mail clerks on the floor as themselves—the "real McCoy"—to tell their own stories using their own words. Brilliant! Many of these men were still alive (the Canadian

Scripted first-person interpretation by two members of the CMC theatre company in the c. 1900 Ontario street of the Museum's Canada Hall. *Photo by: Harry Foster/Steve Darby of Canadian Museum of Civilization*

railway mail service having ended only in 1971), were natural-born raconteurs, and were interested in our project. Why talk about them in the third person when you could involve living members in direct contact with the public? This would be education at its richest: direct access to the people who had lived the experiences and could talk about it first hand. In the end, we didn't do it. The team pulled back from the idea, allowing itself to be stymied by internal roadblocks such as a reluctance by our educator to manage the group of volunteers over the nine-month run of the show. There was fear, as well, of a certain loss of control over what the men would say and how they would behave once set loose in the exhibition gallery. And finally, we were done in by a certain reticence to try an experiment that had never been tried, not at CMC anyway. While the museum had successfully adopted a culture of live interpretation based on theatre, performances, and demonstrations, it had held back from bringing members of a given community into an exhibition space to interact with the public in a conversational, unscripted way.

While the early years of Dramamuse were focused largely on the production of plays, with time the company began experimenting with the idea of first-person characters interacting with the public in a street-theatre way. For this approach David drew inspiration from living history sites in North America and England where it is common to find actor-interpreters 'living' the role of a personage against the backdrop of a real or reconstructed period environment. At CMC the various dwellings along the Canada Hall streetscape provided the ideal theatre set for these role-playing characters. Before too long, a visitor strolling through the Canada Hall was treated to first-person encounters with a host of costumed actors, each playing the part of a character fabricated from a composite of individuals and events from the Canadian past. Gaspard the fur trader leans against a birch-bark canoe in the setting of an early 19th-century fur-trading post and regales passersby with his tales of hair-raising adventures paddling the uncharted waterways of the continent in search of beaver pelts; Rolland the cook, serving up make-believe slop in the setting of a rustic bunkhouse, complains to visitors about the hard life in an Ottawa Valley lumber camp circa 1850; while elegantly attired Mrs. Gordon, matron of a Victorian mansion in small-town Ontario, admonishes her 'house-guests' about the evils of drink and invites visitors back for tea at 4 o'clock (occasionally an unsuspecting visitor will take Mrs. Gordon at her word and return at the appointed hour only to find the actor has gone off duty!).

Schools within the museum's catchment area study the unit, "my community" in grade 4. To introduce their students to the origins of this community of Ottawa-Hull, many local teachers bring their 4th grade classes to the museum to participate in our school programme on the history of lumbering in the Ottawa Valley. The children manipulate living-history artifacts in a touch cart, they make a craft, and they are guided through an exhibition about the place of women during the lumber era. None of these school visits is complete without a trip to the Canada Hall to meet Rolland the cook in his lumber-camp shanty. They gather round his open (simulated) fire in the crudely built bunkhouse and, mesmerized by Rolland's twinkling eyes and gruff, intimate voice, they are transported by his richly detailed tales deep into the primitive forests of the Ottawa Valley a century ago to share in the hard life experienced by the countless men who lived and worked there. Later, as they prepare to board the school bus, the children are on occasion queried about the one aspect they remember most about their visit. Invariably the answer is, the actor. Not only that, they are able to reiterate morsels of historical information that "Rolland" had shared with them. They've learned something. Phew. Mission accomplished. Is it possible that this jovial human spirit with his polished and captivating stories about the past has succeeded to sweeten the medicine of learning, thereby predisposing the children to absorb some of their information-packed visit? Casual observations would suggest as much; however, it merits formal assessment through the vehicle of an evaluation study. Surely, what he has contributed to this school programme is to dramatize a chapter from the past, making it tangible and, as a result, more comprehensible.

David successfully realized the resident theatre company of his vision and guided its pioneering spirit until his sudden and very sad death from a heart attack in June 1995. By then, Dramamuse was an established company of eight actors operating on a full-time, year-round basis, averaging about 55 presentations a week in the two official languages of Canada, English and French. About 30 individual scripts had been developed over the five years, half of which had been translated into the other official language, giving a total of 45 short plays ranging in length from seven to 30 minutes in performance. In addition, the company carried a repertoire of 13 characters used in the first-person interactions (all bilingual) inside the historical environment of the Canada Hall. The company had become an important model for museums around the world to follow. Not bad for five years' labour.

THE PLOT DEVELOPS

Four years later, Dramamuse pushes valiantly onward, expanding on the interactive characters and producing new plays in response to the needs of new exhibitions, in an effort to remain true to the original vision. It is clear that theatre is indeed a powerful interpretive device in the tool box of media employed to convey the messages in an exhibition story line. Not all exhibitions require the involvement of theatre, however. That is a decision to be taken by the exhibition project team as they develop the story line and identify the interpretive methods that can best convey each of the messages. An illustration of this process is provided by the exhibition, *Doukhobors: Spirit Wrestlers,* about the Doukhobor people who fled religious persecution in Russia in the early part of the century and settled in western Canada. A key message the curator wished to convey was the importance of the tradition of song in Doukhobor culture. Rather than convey this message through text, the team (comprised of project manager, designer, curator, interpretive planner, and an advisor from the Doukhobor community) decided audio-visual was a more effective medium and proceeded to commission an elaborate three-screen production that became the physical and conceptual centre of the exhibition. Complemented to this, a local woman of Doukhobor heritage was hired periodically to demonstrate traditional activities such as spinning and cooking, and to speak to visitors about contemporary Doukhobor culture. Finally, the museum's new and able artistic director, Richard Leger, was brought into the process to create a theatre piece for the exhibition. The play *Spirit Singers*, became the museum's first multi-media production, in which the actor's monologue is interwoven with film images projected onto the screens behind her and with sound recordings of Doukhobor song. To be sure, the actor's timing must be impeccable in order to synchronize with these audio-visual elements stored on laser disc. Through this careful orchestration of actor performance with multi-media technology, Richard Leger succeeds in creating a visual metaphor stressing the paradox of Doukhobor identity, in which the actor/character becomes lost among the multitude of faces and voices singing (in true Doukhobor custom).

Today at CMC, work is under way to complete the First Peoples Hall, a permanent installation that surveys the culture and history of Canada's aboriginal peoples, scheduled to open in 2000. In this project we are confronted by the very issue of cultural appropriation addressed back in 1988, that is, whose story is it and who has the right to tell it? The matter of how or, for that matter, whether to incorporate theatre as an interpretive medium in this exhibition gallery, is currently under review. Representatives of Canada's various native communities sit as advisors on the gallery planning team and their counsel will be instrumental in deciding the final form that live interpretation will take in this, the last of the permanent exhibition spaces at CMC to be completed. Over the past two summers we have employed some aboriginal people to animate temporary exhibitions dealing with their own cultural communities. Their task has been to greet visitors, tour them through the exhibitions, and, generally, to speak about contemporary native culture based on their own life experience. Not surprisingly, visitors to the CMC have registered enthusiastic appreciation of this direct form of interpretation. In an institution such as the CMC with a strong ethnocultural focus and the mandate to foster intercultural understanding, it only makes sense to facilitate direct interactions between visitor and community member. No role playing, no script necessary: the community member speaks from first-hand experience.

Theatre has a place, of course, in this interpretive framework, to provide the element of the dramatized past. As well, different visitors to the museum require different interpretive methods. While a casual visitor strolling through the halls may be content to linger in conversation with the First Peoples animator, the school group marching through their 90-minute structured programme requires a script that is to the point and addresses the elements of the curriculum.

We are very fortunate at the CMC to have actors on full-time staff, ensuring that the resident theatre company plays to appreciative audiences in the exhibition halls the year round. However, ten years later, the size of the company is reduced, the rate of new production diminished, and we feel under threat by an administration battered by the need to do more with less in this modern-day, cost-cutting environment brought on by shrinking budgets. Ten years ago, the sky was the limit in terms of both ambition and dollars available. Now, our challenge is to find efficiencies that will minimize behind-the-scenes research and rehearsal time and maximize front-of-house time

playing to the audience that is our *raison d'etre*. We are keenly aware of the need for a "critical mass" of actors on staff, below which number we cannot meet commitments to school programmes, maintain a visibility in the Canada Hall during peak hours, or stage plays such as *Hatshepsut*, an ambitious production incorporated into our 1998 blockbuster, *Mysteries of Egypt* exhibition. Though integrated into the museum's mission on a philosophical level, the security of Dramamuse within the current administrative structure is more precarious. The increasing need to "prove" a programme in terms of performance indicators such as revenue generation is problematic for interpretive theatre whose impact, for the most part, is best measured according to the quality it contributes to the visitor experience. Surely the challenge ahead will be to coin performance indicators that can measure this quality, using a quantitative language that speaks to administrative concerns, including a demonstration of strategic benefits to be reaped.

Intellectually, we continue also to wrestle with the tension inherent between theatre as a self-standing artistic medium guided by its own set of linguistic and behavioural rules, and theatre as one of many interpretive tools employed within an exhibition context. The museological side of this dialectic was captured ten years ago by our director:

"Museums of course are not in the business of professional theatre. . . . Their educational mission, the presence of authentic icons rather than just props, and their preoccupation with heritage and cultural ritual, must inevitably influence the types of dramatic productions . . . " (MacDonald, 1989:177).

A decade later, this is where we stand. A little less starry-eyed, a lot more world-wise, but the belief in the power of theatre as a means of communication within a museum context remains as strong and fervent as ever.

We know that theatre enhances the visitor experience by stimulating interest in and response to our exhibits; by provoking excitement and reaction; by contextualizing information; by helping to show that museum interpretation is just that, interpretation; and by providing a fun and entertaining time that will encourage repeat visits. We have included a theatre experience in each of our special-audience programmes, knowing that it's both a key ingredient in making the visit special and a value-added feature that sets us apart from competing museums in the region.

As the eyes of the school children gaze transfixed upon Madame Aubry gently rolling the flowers of a flax plant between her fingers as she explains in her thick Old World accent the manufacture of linen back in the days of New France, there is no doubt in our minds that interpretive theatre at the CMC is the best thing going.

BIBLIOGRAPHY

Blais, Jean-Marc (ed.), The Languages of Live Interpretation: Animation in Museums, Canadian Museum of Civilization Mercury Series, Directorate Paper 9, 1997.

MacDonald, George and Alsford, Stephen, A Museum for the Global Village (Canadian Museum of Civilization: Hull, 1989).

Alsford, Stephen and Parry, David, 'Interpretive theatre: a role in museums', Museum Management and Curatorship 10 1991: 8-23.

Cannizzo, Jeanne and Parry, David, 'Museum theatre in the 1990s: trail-blazer or camp-follower?, in Pearce, Susan (ed.), Museums and the Appropriation of Culture, Athlone Press, London, 1994.

Hudson, Kenneth, A Social History of Museums: What the Visitors Thought, MacMillan Press Ltd., London, 1975.

Parry, David and Boucher, Louise, Live Interpretation at the Canadian Museum of Civilization: A Policy Proposal, unpublished manuscript, 1988.

Parry, David, "Interpretive Theatre, Spring-Summer 1994", unpublished manuscript, 1994.

RESPONSE TO *Theater as Integral Force*

JULIE I. JOHNSON
NEW JERSEY STATE AQUARIUM, DIRECTOR OF EDUCATION

The education department at the New Jersey State Aquarium is responsible for the development and delivery of all exhibit-based programs, school on-site and outreach efforts, teacher training, family workshops, sleep overs, and camp programs. We employ a variety of modes when developing programs in order to reach the largest number of visitors.

Similar to the experiences of the Canadian Museum of Civilization, the aquarium has found that theater engages the audience quickly and keeps them enthralled. When audience participation is included, the results are even better. Theater is not for everyone and some patrons prefer the science demonstrations or traditional presentations. Our experience does show, however, that this mode works quite well for family audiences.

The history of theater at the aquarium actually started prior to its opening in 1992. In collaboration with Glassboro State College's theater department, the aquarium produced The Riverkeepers: The Adventures of Allie the Shad, a traveling theater program funded by the Geraldine R. Dodge Foundation. This initial form of school outreach was seen by more than 25,000 students in the Pennsylvania-New Jersey-Delaware region. Students and teachers alike enjoyed the different format. Students were able to "get" the messages in the play as evidenced by follow-up evaluation. Due to our experience with Allie, there was no doubt that theater could be used successfully by the aquarium to teach science-related concepts.

The next opportunity to incorporate theater occurred when the traveling exhibit, What About Whales?, came to the aquarium in the spring of 1993. During the planning of programs to support the temporary exhibit, one staff member with a background in theater suggested a play. Whale Song, written by a playwright at the Walnut Street Theater in Philadelphia, became the next venture into the realm of educational theater. This time the audience was the general visitor. Professional actors were hired on a part-time basis for the run of the show. Again, exit interviews with visitors confirmed our earlier experience. Subsequent aquarium in-house programs included a number of summer productions performed by a mixture of professional part-time actors and education staff members with a flare for drama.

In May 1996, the theater aspect of the education department was formalized in the form of the Drama Gills, the aquarium's theater troupe. This was an extension and refinement of our nontraditional format for providing educational experiences to general visitors and through our outreach program.

At present, the Drama Gills perform on site, year-round, delivering short vignettes as well as 25-30 minute theater pieces. They also perform as the Clamshell Traveling Theater Program, the outreach component targeted at schools, church, and community groups that want something other than a traditional classroom-based outreach experience.

The troupe consists of six to eight part-time professional actors/actresses and one full-time coordinator, each with a strong background in theater and a combined total of more than 25 years experience in children's theater. The theater pieces are written by troupe members who bring complex science concepts to life. Dramatic and comedic formats are used as vehicles to provide educational experiences for a variety of audiences.

Ideas for the shows and vignettes come from folk tales, children's stories, and even Shakespeare. Sometimes a particular science concept is the motivation for a piece and the actors work from there to begin writing. All longer pieces include positive personal reinforcements through the use of story morals to teach aquatic animal behavior in a humorous and entertaining fashion.

Since the theater troupe at NJSA is part of the education department, programs developed for other areas also benefit from the actors' knowledge and talents. The theater coordinator assists with the development of demos and presentations. This past year, our sleep-over program was developed and implemented by a team of staff including three of the actors. The perspective that the actors bring to any program planning process is always refreshing.

Because the aquarium uses part-time labor for its theater troupe, turnover and scheduling can be a challenge. The actors are professionals working in the field and sometimes their external commitments keep them away for long periods of time. On the plus side, the fluid nature of the group means that no one gets bored with performing the same thing day in and day out.

Currently, general operating and sponsorship funds support the troupe. The ability to expand the troupe and/or make positions full time will depend on future availability of funds and the continued success of the program.

CHAPTER 5

STAFFING

John Fulweiler, Past Coordinator of Wildlife Theater
Central Park Wildlife Center, New York

Wildlife Theater is performed in the Central Park Zoo located in the heart of New York City: theater capital of the United States. Here, one small ad for actors in *Backstage* produces about 700 resumes. Your applicant pool may be different from ours, as will your institution and the theater program you create for it. However, we will both find certain casting truths to be self-evident, whether we are hiring students or professionals, for a zoo or a museum, anywhere in America or the world.

As the producer and director of Wildlife Theater for the last three years, I went through the casting process three times. The process evolved each year, as the program itself evolved. This paper identifies some of the idiosyncrasies of casting in an institutional setting, some things to look for and some things to avoid. Included are the methods used in casting Wildlife Theater, as well as some thoughts on how other institutions might proceed.

WHERE TO START

HIRE A DIRECTOR

Everything from the look of the show to the actors' movements and placement (blocking) is under the ultimate control of the director. You will still determine your institution's message, but you will need a professional director to craft that message into effective performances—and to coordinate casting.

ACTORS: EDUCATION STAFF, VOLUNTEERS, OR PAID ACTORS?

You will need to decide who will perform your programming: in-house education staff, volunteers, or paid actors. Each has their own merits and drawbacks.

VOLUNTEERS

Volunteers are not used in Wildlife Theater. I have, however, trained volunteers for off-season sea lion feeding narrations. These performances require presentational skills, but not necessarily theatrical training. Out of approximately 100 volunteers, perhaps 30 had an initial interest in learning the narration. Of these, some developed stage fright or bowed out for other reasons. Currently, nine volunteers participate in the program; these few enjoy it and their contributions are valuable. It should be noted, however, that none of the volunteers delivered as professional a narration as our actors, who are used during the regular season.

We should also realize that volunteers share their valuable time with institutions for various reasons, but not necessarily to do theater. At Central Park Zoo, none of them had any notion of acting when they signed on. In planning a theater program, ask yourself if you want to require acting from volunteers—for most people a terrifying prospect. Or, even more sticky, will they all be allowed to act? Quality control can become an issue.

If you decide to use your volunteers as performers I suggest that you take their time, feelings, and thoughts about your new program—and their place in it—into consideration first.

Here is another idea: hire a volunteer acting troupe, one dedicated solely to the theatrical side of your institution's interpretive goals. The up side is that even actors in training will readily understand the language and mechanics of theater. It would mean that all volunteer actors would know exactly what they were volunteering for, with clearly defined benefits and expectations defined from the outset. Quality control would be addressed in the selection process, avoiding the risk of hurting the feelings of valuable volunteers already on your staff. The possible down side is the fact that volunteers are seldom held to as rigid a schedule as paid staff, and this won't work with a theater program. The show must go on. Similarly, unless you are starting with a weekend-only program, you may have to hire multiple actors to fill a daily schedule. Each new actor needs to be directed into the show and time must be allowed for the director to do so. Where actors are available, such as New York City, you will not get the best actors without pay. Still hiring a volunteer troupe might be a way to try out theater as a concept in your institution.

EDUCATION STAFF

The decision to use education staff as actors is usually based on: (i) a belief that teaching has theatrical elements not far removed from acting; (ii) the hope that money can be saved by not hiring additional staff; (iii) the fear that actors—or anyone from outside—will alter the purity of the educational message.

It is true that good teachers possess skills useful to actors—and many teachers can become actors with training. But make no mistake—training will be essential. Acting is a skill just as is teaching. Does your staff have time for the training they will need—let alone time for performing shows? Who will provide the training?

PAID ACTORS

Wildlife Theater employs 14 actors (in addition to the coordinator), who are all paid professionals. From my experience, hiring actors is the way to go and here is why:

- Actors Are Cost Effective. Teachers and other staff are full-time employees, with benefits and higher pay than the hourly actors you will be hiring initially. Why take your valuable staff from the jobs they are trained to do when for less money experienced professionals can be hired?

- Actors Are Messengers. There is no need to worry about actors getting your message wrong. Your organization—not the actors—will determine the content of your programming. Think of the actors as mailmen, hired to deliver your message—not to write it.

- Actors Are Professionals. Everyone working at your institution was carefully selected for their experience and educational background. Why hold theater—or any program (particularly any public program)—to a lesser standard? Starting small in size is fine; compromising quality is not. Hire good actors, even if you only hire a few.

See Appendix B. for sample position descriptions.

SOME PLACES TO LOOK FOR ACTORS:

- Newspapers. Ads in the help wanted section may get results.

- Professional Publications. Backstage is published in New York City and lists casting for New York as well as regional theaters casting in New York; some other large cities have similar publications.

- Community Theaters. Many cities have a resident theater company. You can request that they put up your casting notices.

- Schools. Universities and colleges (even high schools) usually have some kind of theater program, particularly useful for seasonal hires.

A NOTE ON UNIONS: ACTORS EQUITY

There are several trade unions for actors. The union you will deal with most often, since it covers stage actors, is Actors Equity. An actor who is a member of this union is largely prohibited from accepting acting work in shows or theaters not under contract with Equity. A union actor can take advantage of various remedies if they wish to work at your institution, most of them involving permission from Equity. Adherence to these rules is the responsibility of each actor, but it is important to state your union affiliation or lack thereof from the beginning. Many quality actors can be found with no union affiliation. If you have questions, you should call the union representative in your region.

THE CASTING NOTICE

A casting notice should include:

- Your institution's name and address;

- What each applicant should send (a picture and resume);

- An indication of 'Pay' or 'No Pay' only, stating clearly your union affiliation, union contract, or lack thereof;

- Perhaps a line on the specific skills you value and seek;

- A request that applicants neither call nor visit.

THE AUDITION

There are many ways to audition actors, but always bear in mind that the audition—which actors correctly view as an unpaid performance—is your first interaction with your potential troupe. Know what you need to see, make a realistic audition schedule, and stick to it.

STEP ONE: THE INITIAL AUDITION

Go through the resumes you receive, noting any educational theater or work in your discipline, contact applicants you wish to see, and give them the following:

- time and location (plus directions);

- What they need to prepare. Actors usually prepare one to two short monologues, either contemporary or classic, dramatic or comedic, as well as songs. However, prepared material is not necessary. You must state what you would like to see;

- What each applicant should wear, for example, loose clothing, etc. (note: you can tell a lot by the appropriateness of an applicant's attire);

- A contact number to confirm appointment times.

You will need a large room for the audition and at least one person to assist with the mechanics of the audition (keeping actors' head shots straight, handling actors as they arrive, etc.). As a spirit of collegiality and inclusion are necessary elements to the success of any new program, I urge you to allow members of your institution's staff to attend, as observers, any or all of the auditions. Staff who observed the auditions at the CPZ gained insight into the theatrical process and found themselves reassured by the skill and professionalism of the people who would be delivering their message to the public. The actors, for their part, gained an insight into the institution they hoped to be working for.

WHAT DO YOU LOOK FOR?

A bad monologue—or even a good one, for that matter—can hide an actor's strengths and/or weaknesses. Instead, I use improvisational games in the initial audition. An example of one is "Animal Party." Each actor picks a favorite animal. Then the director explains that each actor will assume the characteristics of the animal they have chosen—its physicality, size, diet, even imagined spiritual or emotional characteristics. The actors will not be animals—but people with the characteristics of these animals. You can suggest examples to the actors: "He's like a bull in a china shop," "She's stubborn as a mule," etc. They are then told they will be attending a birthday party. The director picks one actor to be the birthday boy or girl. This actor begins the scene and the director signals each actor to enter in character.

Your director will know other theater games as well, or you can pick up a copy of Viola Spolin's Theater Games or Keith Johnstone's Impro. Both are excellent.

The director may give directions to the actors during the audition; note whether or not an actor takes them readily and effectively. Pay attention to everything: the actor's vocal quality, entertainment skills, and even his or her fearlessness to play a scene like "Animal Party" which they may never have played before. This is not a regular acting job; adaptability is invaluable. Call back anyone who does something you think is special. This past season I auditioned about 170 actors and called back 34—one in five.

STEP TWO: THE CALL BACK

Your requirements for the call back will vary depending on your program. For Wildlife Theater the actors were asked to:

- Read from sides—brief excerpts of dialogue—from the shows;

- Use puppets in a scene;

- Sing a verse of Old McDonald, just to make sure each actor could carry a tune and convey the meaning of the song.

After you have seen everything you need to see, explain the pay scale, the hours to be worked, and the projected season dates, if any. Ask the actors whether they can work the shifts as described. Some will bow out at this point. Choose your finalists; it's time for the interview.

STEP THREE: THE INTERVIEW

In the acting world, interviews are not common. Before the end of the first season, however, it became apparent that interviews would have been helpful. This is not simply an acting job; it's a season-long commitment with unique requirements, not all of them defined by performance skill. When casting you have the right—and the absolute need—to know where the applicants are coming from.

Invite each finalist to interview with you on the phone or in your office. What you talk about depends on what you feel you need to know. Open all the closets. Allow the candidates plenty of latitude in their responses; get to know them. Here are some sample questions asked of Central Park Zoo applicants:

- What specifically prompted you to respond to our casting notice? (Many actors audition for everything, which is commendable—but you don't need actors who want any acting job, you need actors who want this acting job—and you can find them.)

- Do you like children? Animals? What do you like about them? (An astonishing number of applicants felt they could perform for children effectively without liking them, and on behalf of wildlife without caring about animals. For a few weeks, perhaps, but by the Fourth of July? No way.)

- If Francis Ford Coppola and I each offered you an acting job—and we could both pay the same wages—which job would you take? Why?

- Do you believe we can make a difference in the public's attitudes towards the natural world?

- Is the pay for this job agreeable to you?

STEP FOUR: CHOOSE YOUR COMPANY

Describe the job in detail to your candidates one last time making sure they understand the special needs of this unique acting job. Do not hire until and unless you get a definite, enthusiastic acceptance. No matter how talented an actor may be, there is simply no substitute for enthusiasm.

CONCLUSION

After 17 years as an actor and three seasons at the Central Park Zoo, I urge you to bear two things in mind when casting:

First, a theater troupe can never be better than the actors in it. Money spent on sets, costumes, or puppets is money wasted if quality actors are not found, hired, and nurtured. You are entrusting your educational message to these performers—and, moreover, they will become the face of your institution.

Second, make sure the space you create for your actors is not separate from the life of your institution. Find ways to facilitate synergy between docents, volunteers, education staff, and actors. Bring them into the culture of your organization. The actors of Wildlife Theater have expanded the Central Park Zoo's public programs. The Central Park Zoo has in turn expanded the actors' horizons; they now discuss various animals and read about wildlife at breaks and even take books home for further study. The Central Park Zoo and the actors who perform there have reached each other with the same generosity we aspire to in reaching the public we serve: a noble goal for any public institution.

RESPONSE TO *Staffing*

TRACY MACMORINE, EXHIBIT PROGRAM COORDINATOR—CAST THEATRE PROGRAM
CINCINNATI MUSEUM CENTER

In response to the chapter on staffing actors by John Fulweiler, Theater Specialist at the Central Park Zoo, I agree with and support virtually everything he says. Hiring professional theater artists (actors and directors) is the most efficient way to build a successful museum theater program. Museum Center's CAST Theatre Program is run in a contrasting manner, however, so I'll highlight some of our differences and similarities based on Fulweiler's outline.

A. WHERE TO START

1. HIRE A DIRECTOR

Absolutely, the director must be a theater professional. I, as coordinator, came into my position with no museum experience—but with a strong background in directing, creative dramatics, and educational theater. I direct most of the shows, but usually once a year I hire a guest director—always a theater professional with whose work I'm familiar.

2. ACTORS

a. Student Actors, the Basics

The CAST actors are all students, ages 14-18, who are seriously considering careers in theater. They volunteer their time for meetings and rehearsals, but are paid for all performances. Pay starts at minimum wage (currently $5.15 an hour) with a 10 cent annual step-up based on both merit and participation.

During the school-year, performances take place on weekends as well as winter and spring breaks. Summertime performances run six days per week. While currently this limits us from performing for school groups and other week-day visitors, it's feasible that the program could expand by tapping into the increasing population of home-schooled students.

b. Why Hire Students?

Museum Center is dedicated to youth programs that are designed to encourage and support each student as he or she explores, discovers, creates, invents, learns, and shares the skills acquired with peers, staff, and our visitors. Our youth programs provide a working experience for high school students, make use of their interests in a variety of subjects, and promote and enhance their path to university study.

c. Adult Volunteers

While adult volunteers are not involved with CAST, I have hired them in the past for a short-term theater project: as "volunterrors" in our BOOFEST Haunted Neighborhood. Although some (maybe 10 percent) volunterrors did an excellent job with lines, costumes, and make-up (provided by us), enthusiasm, and delivery, I would not depend on them for future theatrical events for many of the reasons that Fulweiler pointed out: last minute stage fright, quality control of performances, and scheduling issues—rampant absenteeism!

d. Volunteer Acting Troupes

The most successful volunterror shifts were filled by high school drama clubs (different from the individual students hired for CAST shows). Upon receiving the scripts, their directors assigned parts and gave them time to practice. I went to each of the participating schools for only one rehearsal. The enthusiasm, mixed with the perceived structure of a school-sanctioned yet 'grown-up' activity resulted in crowd-pleasing performances, punctual actor check-ins, and no absenteeism.

Unfortunately, the adult volunteer acting troupes that signed up for volunterror shifts left much to be desired. Egos ruled, rehearsals were met with disdain, and punctuality, even showing up for the shift, seemed to be optional. Obviously, this lack of discipline is not acceptable in an institution—is it anywhere? Perhaps other adult volunteer acting troupes would be more reliable, but the ones that responded to our recruitment efforts were not.

B. FINDING ACTORS

1. TEACHER MAILINGS

Three times a year I do a mailing to both the theater director and English department head of each high school and middle school in the greater Cincinnati area. The mailing should include a letter to the educator, explaining the opportunity available to their students and asking them for their help by encouraging prospective actors and posting an audition flier.

An audition flier—eye catching, usually on fluorescent paper, with just the basic information:

- Student Auditions headline

- The date, place, and time, and a teaser

- "You even GET PAID for Performances!"

An application must be turned in at the audition. Besides the basic information, I ask for all regularly scheduled commitments (to troubleshoot scheduling conflicts) as well as two personality revealing essays—this somewhat takes the place of Fulweiler's interview.

I also supply an in-depth Audition Information Sheet, which discusses show content, available roles, audition requirements, and all rehearsal, performance, and administrative commitments.

2. NEWSPAPER ANNOUNCEMENTS

Audition notices are posted free of charge in our local paper on Friday and Saturday. I generally start having them run two weeks prior to the audition date.

C. THE AUDITION

I schedule auditions four people to a half-hour block. Usually, they are required to:

- Perform a memorized one-to-two-minute monologue, poem, or story—this tells me right away if they've put forth any effort, as well as showing stage presence and movement patterns.

- Teach the group a simple game, song, or activity that has motions to it—I want to see how they are at taking a familiar concept, breaking it down into steps, and communicating those steps to others.

- Improvise with others in the group—I need to see how they interact in structured situations.

- Show off any special talents—you never know what people are capable of (magic tricks, acrobatics, sword-swallowing). This really lets the actor's personality shine through!

D. CHOOSING THE COMPANY

Our shows are all triple-cast (the only way to work with teen schedules) based on the audition and application. Separate auditions are held for each show, so the student's initial time commitment is only three and a half months—one month of rehearsal and 10 weekends of performance. Thus, if I've accidentally cast a "stinker" they're only around for a short while. Those who prove themselves to be responsible, enthusiastic, and talented are encouraged to re-audition each time.

E. CONCLUSION

Whether involving student actors or professional adult actors, I whole-heartedly agree with Fulweiler's conclusion that actors will flourish if given the space and that this space must be integral to the life of the institution. If treated as only a fringe group, the relationship becomes unbalanced. Institutions must serve the actors if they expect the actors to keep service to the institution a top priority.

CHAPTER 6

TURNING AN ACTOR INTO AN INTERPRETER

Andrew Ashmore, Actors' Company Manager
Museum of the Moving Image, London

The Museum of the Moving Image opened in September 1988. It was the first museum in the United Kingdom to use first-person interpretation on a large scale and guarantee 100 percent visitor contact. Any visitor will encounter six actors as they tour the museum. The museum employs 18 actors and three animation assistants on 21-week contracts, which break down into 18 weeks on the galleries, preceded by an intensive research and rehearsal programme lasting three weeks.

The company won a National Training Award in 1989 for this training programme, which has steadily been augmented and improved over the years. This article gives a little more information on what it takes to transform an actor into a first-person interpreter.

1. INTAKE

Before any actor starts the first day of training, he or she will have had to get through several stages of a carefully structured recruitment process. The initial advertisement requires photo, curriculum vitae or resume, and cover letter including reasons why the actor wants to work in our particular environment. Group auditions test not only acting ability, but also speed and articulacy of improvisation and, crucially, generosity of spirit and sensitivity to others. We do not look for 'traditional thespians' but recognise that working on the galleries requires strong interpersonal and communication skills, and an element of the educator as well as performer. (See Appendix D. Information Leaflet)

We see around 80-100 new actors for the 18 vacancies, while a figure of 10-15 actors wishing to return for another contract is not uncommon. The auditions are broken into two sections: an initially large group working through a number of improvisation games and exercises; and a smaller subsection selected after a break then working in-depth on speeches and character improvisation work. The full audition lasts around two and a half hours.

An in-depth interview follows a few days later, which assesses the actor's perceptions of the job and its requirements and challenges, their capacity for research, their prior knowledge of/interest in their subject (we ask for preferences to work in different areas of the museum, which are taken into account at casting), and stresses the need for team work. At the end of an exhausting seven or eight days for company manager and director the selection is made and training can begin.

2. TRAINING

The three-week rehearsal period is very intensive and benefits from having a few ex-company members on board. It is gratifying that actors want to return to work here again (the record is six contracts!), and their confidence and experience certainly help the first-time actors. Ex-actors are also used by the director to help in rehearsal sessions where they interpret an area of the museum in which they have worked before—although they are encouraged to take on at least one new area within the museum and to develop a different character with a whole new biography if they are in the same area again.

The areas our characters inhabit are as follows: 1896 'Pre-Cinema'-actor telling the story of developments up to the arrival of the cinematograph (demonstrates optical toys and operates Magic Lantern and Theatre Optique); Electric Palace—early cinema owner, c. 1916 welcomes audiences to a most palatial environment and exhibits the latest releases; 1927 Hollywood Casting Director—always on the lookout for fresh talent while sharing the stories and scandals of the stars; Russian Agit-Train—Bolshevik agitator tells tales of Revolution and narrates films by Eisenstein, Pudovkin, and Vertov; Hollywood 1939—Hollywood Director conducts screen tests on the studio set and has news of all the latest movies; 1946 Odeon—a commissionaire and usherette ensure good behaviour and decency in the flagship cinema chain of the period. Each actor will play two characters, alternating between the two on a weekly basis.

Actors on Agitational Propaganda Train (Bolshevik Revolutionaries c. 1917) are (left to right) Mark Pentecost, Stephanie Jackson (standing front), Anna Wynnyczuk (standing rear), Kevin Exley. *Photograph by Kevin Martin. Photo courtesy of Museum of the Moving Image*

In order to play any of these parts convincingly and be able to respond to the need for information from our visitors, there is some serious preparatory work to be done. After being accepted, each actor collects research packs compiled here at the museum which contain information on both social and film history relating to the period they will represent. This is a starting point for research, and does not constitute the full amount of information required for their characters. (See Appendix D. Actors' Research Material)

In addition to the research packs, we also have a well-stocked library in our education department for the actors to use. It comprises both books and videos relating to all areas of the museum.

Formal structured training is centred around character rehearsals with the director, designed to give each actor

the knowledge and confidence to work on the galleries with confidence and conviction. These sessions include a Russian lesson for our Bolsheviks, general character work and group exercises, and revolve around skill-sharing and polling information on a wide variety of topics, as individual actors research independently and then share their findings with the group. Actors also receive seminars from outside experts on their area, have a scheduled big-screen showing of a seminal movie or movies from the period, a series of lectures on the galleries and exhibits, talks from members of the curatorial team and departments such as education, press and marketing, technical, and front of house rounded off with general sessions on health and safety, disability awareness, and museum operations and procedures.

An important part of the rehearsal process takes place on the galleries, either before the museum opens or after it has closed. This helps the actors utilise the theoretical knowledge they have gained, combined with the character they have created, in the environment in which they will be working.

Hands-on sessions include coaching on how to operate the museum's Magic Lantern and Theatre Optique, narrating a film section as it plays on the screen in specific areas, and song and dance or comedy routines in the Odeon—all in front of the director and other actors. (See Appendix D. Actors' Preparation Sessions)

The song and dance or comedy routine will be in 1940s style using original material and is designed to cover the rewind of the museum's tour compilation of film extracts, when for six to seven minutes, there is nothing on screen in the museum's cinema.

3. ON THE GALLERIES

Although the training is both intensive and detailed, we recognise that there are many things that an actor can learn only through direct experience on the galleries. One of the first training sessions involves a talk about the history and development of Theatre-in-Museum, and then a group discussion highlighting any concerns the actor may have about working in this environment. By holding this session at the outset, and having ex-actors present to contribute their experiences, the choices the actors will make regarding their characters and approach to work over the period of training are more likely to be choices that will enable them to work at maximum efficacy in the museum.

During their first four weeks on the galleries, the actors are coached and appraised by the director and company manager, and given regular feedback sessions on what they are doing well and what could be improved on. The need to research continually throughout the term of the contract is stressed; knowledge is fuel both in terms of varying delivery and content of material and also building confidence with visitors. Having said that, on the galleries, it is often the actor who sets the agenda, although a skilled interpreter will blend leading and following quite seamlessly. (See Appendix D. Guidelines)

At the end of the fourth week on the floor, each actor will sit down with the director for a structured assessment and feedback session (this also corresponds with the end of the probation period built into the contract). From then on they are largely unsupervised, but encouraged to continually challenge themselves and develop as interpreters. Individual responsibility and team professionalism are the bywords. The company manager is also present on a daily basis both to support the actors and channel their feedback from the museum and its visitors to the wider curatorial and technical team, and also to supervise their activities and co-ordinate involvement in other projects not directly connected to the day-to-day running of the museum. Of which there are now many, ranging from educational workshops to new exhibition launches, for departments as diverse as education and corporate development.

As well as the core work on the galleries, performances featuring the actors' company in recent months have included Eisenstein in Action—a full length play recreating the master classes at the Moscow Film School given by the great director; an evening with Lord Reith, founder of the BBC; and Following Frankenstein's Footsteps—an evening blending the acting skills of four of the company with archival footage of the enduring movie monster.

Actors on Hollywood Studios 1927 and 1939 are (left to right) John Gregor, Paul Hurstfield, Premi Mowli, Paul Rogan, George Eggay (seated). Photograph by Kevin Martin. *Photo courtesy of Museum of the Moving Image*

4. CONCLUSION

Market research has consistently shown how highly valued our interpreters are by our visitors. This comes from the actors' combination of passion for their subject and the ability to communicate information about it. Their role is to educate, inform, and entertain so that our visitors learn through interaction. The intensive training period gives the actor a strong foundation and solid framework within which to operate. Support and feedback on the galleries flesh this out still further. So that, seamlessly, the transition has been made—the actor has become an interpreter.

RESPONSE TO *Turning an Actor into an Interpreter*

SIMONE MORTAN, MONTEREY BAY AQUARIUM

The Monterey Bay Aquarium visitor programs department offers a variety of programs in and around the aquarium. For the purpose of responding to Andrew Ashmore's chapter, I will rely on examples from our summer program season. During the busy summer months the level of our programming rises dramatically with the addition of 11 daily "deck shows" and entertainment for visitors while they wait in line to enter the aquarium. This year our deck shows include: Sea Styles Fashion Show, a tongue-in-cheek fashion show providing an introduction to habitats using larger-than-life costumes featuring animals from various habitats in Monterey Bay; Collecting for Monterey Bay Aquarium, a SCUBA dress-up program that explains SCUBA diving equipment and other tools used to collect animals for the aquarium; and Tide Pool Diver, a program that uses large puppets and live animals to introduce our audience to three different animals and the near-shore habitats where they live. The "Greeters" at the front of the aquarium use larger-than-life costumes to engage visitors in brief improvisational conversations with the goal of introducing visitors to the idea of habitats and what they might expect to see once inside the aquarium.

RECRUITMENT

I agree completely with Andrew Ashmore's comment that ". . . working on the galleries requires strong interpersonal and communication skills, and an element of the educator as well as performer."

The staff for our summer programs are paid college interns. The interview/audition process we follow is not as extensive as that described by Ashmore. We conduct a more traditional interview with an eye out for qualities such as enthusiasm and interest in the marine environment. We look for candidates who have had experiences such as school or community drama, teaching, coaching, or other opportunities for public presentation. The last part of our interview is more audition, in that we have the candidate dress up in one of our animal costumes and do a cold reading of a brief script they might use to interact with visitors waiting in line. This gives us the chance to see if they are willing to experiment with movement in costume and how quickly they can find a voice for an animal character. In our use of animal costumes we strive to provide visitors with a nugget of factual information about the animal and the habitat it lives in. It is important that we do not overly anthropomorphize the animals.

Some of our candidates are attending school too distant to come in for a face-to-face interview. Then we must rely on phone interviews and "cold readings" over the phone. If a candidate makes it into the finalist pool on the basis of a phone interview, we request that they send us a video of a public presentation or a reading of a script that we send them.

TRAINING

Training for our summer interns takes place during an intensive two-week period. The first few days focus on content with an introduction to the aquarium and the marine science background information they will need to answer the most common questions. We also devote time to customer-service training and team building. The remainder of the training has a focus on basic and applied theater skills. The last few days are devoted to time in small groups rehearsing scripts and learning how to move in costumes and use props.

ON THE DECK AND IN FRONT OF THE AQUARIUM

Like the Museum of the Moving Image, we recognize that training must continue once our summer staff begin the public presentation of their programs. This takes the form of constant feedback on performances and optional enrichment activities.

Initially this feedback comes from our permanent staff who make time in their schedules to view several shows each day during the first two weeks of summer programs. In addition, we have one summer intern who has returned for a second year in a mentoring capacity. The mentor is responsible for additional feedback, modeling, and scheduling. Finally, as the season progresses, each day one member of the summer staff gets the opportunity to observe programs and provide feedback at our daily afternoon debriefing. We find this monitoring by peers is perhaps the most valuable feedback. Each staff person gets the chance to view programs with a critical eye. When providing this feedback we always try to find positive notes to share about each performance as well as zero in on finer details that can be improved for future performances. We have repeatedly seen the fruits of this type of feedback when something that "works" in one performance, a gesture or use of a puppet, an improvisational change of wording, is then adopted by other staff members and implemented with the overall effect being constant improvement of everyone's programs.

Andrew Ashmore comments that "individual responsibility and team professionalism" are bywords. In our summer programs teamwork and professionalism are vital to success. In addition to the team building sessions during our two weeks of intensive training, we have daily morning and afternoon briefing (30 minute) sessions. The morning sessions cover daily assignments and scheduling and always end with warm-up exercises before beginning a day of performing. These exercises can be improv games, voice warm-ups, or physical stretching exercises. The afternoon sessions are a time to discuss needs such as costume or prop repairs, and provide the time for giving and receiving feedback. Our summer staff enthusiastically support these daily sessions and comment that they are instrumental in developing strong team identity.

FURTHER ENRICHMENTS

After the intensive two weeks of training, we provide many optional enrichment training opportunities throughout the summer. Because our summer staff are almost all college interns with plans to pursue careers in marine science or aquarium work, we try to provide them with many opportunities to shadow permanent aquarium employees working outside of visitor programs. We also bring in guest speakers after work hours to give enrich-

ments on topics that will benefit the summer interns. These enrichments serve to broaden their knowledge of the aquarium and the marine environments around Monterey Bay. In turn, they share their enthusiasm with visitors and thus provide even better visitor experiences.

CONCLUSION

Unlike Andrew Ashmore, we do not start out with actors. Our college interns come to us with varying degrees of theater experience. By the end of the summer season, however, they have a foundation of theatrical skills that not only enables them to be fine interpreters, but that will also serve them well in any future positions where public speaking is required.

CHAPTER 7

BUDGETING FOR THEATER

Kathleen F. Wagner
Senior Vice President for Education, Philadelphia Zoo

TREEHOUSE AT THE PHILADELPHIA ZOO

The Philadelphia Zoo's theater troupe is based in the Treehouse—a historic animal building adapted for reuse as an educational playground with seven larger-than-life fiberglass animal habitats for children to climb on and in and learn from. Our design team adapted the building as a giant stage set, with structures such as a five-foot long bird's egg, which encouraged young children to role play and create shows of their own. (Early evaluation showed that children were role-playing, although not to the extent we had hoped.) Paid interns, hired for their knowledge of wildlife biology and education, facilitated the learning experience, in the absence of interpretive labels and a structured program. Over time our interpretive strategy matured into a more structured, more theatrical approach, and today, a troupe of five full-time actors performs hourly, engaging children (and their parents, too) in discovering natural history concepts among the "habitat" stage sets. Actor/educators are now recruited primarily for their acting ability and their skill at working with children—a knowledge of science is a great plus, but not a requirement. Training fills in the gaps.

In addition to the hourly presentations described above for casual visitors to the facility, the troupe also uses theater as an interpretive strategy for structured programs: fee-based school classes, outreach shows, family workshops, educational birthday parties, and overnights (which make Treehouse a profit center for the Zoo!). Other programs such as the seasonal stage show *Wildlife Theater and ZooTales*—short performances at exhibits—are offered by the troupe at no cost for visitors elsewhere in the zoo, offering another, unusual way to learn science at the zoo.

SOURCES OF FUNDING

Now let's take a look at how we fund all this activity. Developing a budget and establishing a funding strategy for a museum theater troupe may seem like a pretty straightforward task—but my hunch is that for most of us, it's anything but straightforward. For example, during its ten-year history, our Philadelphia Zoo troupe has been funded by a combination of grants and operating support, with the balance currently shifting to the operating budget. A local foundation willingly supported start-up efforts, and special programs have also been funded by grants, but most foundations and donors are unwilling to support ongoing programs. They see these expenses—and I believe, correctly—as operating expenses more appropriately included in the organization's annual budget. Our strategy has been to support basic ongoing expenses for our theater program through the zoo's operating budget and to seek grant funds for special projects. Program fees are an important source of operating revenue at the Philadelphia Zoo, and our Treehouse Troupe generates 100 percent of its operating budget through program fees.

FOUNDATION GRANTS

Foundation grants may be the best way to launch a new museum theater program, since a grant-funded program won't add to your museum's overhead. A short-term project, funded by others, may give you a chance to prove the value of theater as an interpretive strategy and develop a realistic budget to present as an operating expense with your departmental budget.

Foundation grants can also serve special audiences and supplement an existing repertoire with a new production, but probably can't reliably serve as the basis for your entire production budget. Corporate sponsorships, on the other hand, can and do provide on-going funding for those museums lucky enough to have garnered this type of support. Your institution's development office, if you have one, is your best resource for identifying appropriate sources of contributed income for your programs. If your museum's development staff can't help you, you can still pursue grants on your own, of course, and the more you know about the foundation world, the better your chances.

As a nonprofit organization, your museum is eligible for a grant award from private, corporate, government, or community foundations. Grants are awarded for specific programs or exhibits, operating expenses, and capital projects. Valuable information on foundations in the United States, their giving interests, amount of grants, deadlines, and foundation name and address can be found in *The Foundation Directory*, published by The Foundation Center, New York, New York. *The Foundation Directory* also provides information on the amount of funding awarded to organizations for programs, so check there to make sure you're targeting the right source. The 1998 edition contains 8,642 entries on individual foundations. If your museum doesn't have a copy of this resource, check your library. The Foundation Center also maintains a Web site at http://www.fdncenter.org

Smaller, local foundations may have a greater incentive to invest in your program, they may be more flexible in their requirements and deadlines, and they may already be familiar with your institution. In Philadelphia, we've received funding from two local private foundations for theater programs. We've also received federal and state grants, and recommend that you consider these sources as well, but be forewarned that the application forms are challenging and the process often lengthy.

Federal grants are usually extremely competitive, although they offer a high level of support, so may be well worth the rigorous and complex application process. In Philadelphia, we've been successful at including theater as a component of a larger, more comprehensive federal grant, but have not sought federal grants for theater alone. The National Endowment for the Humanities funded exhibit interpretation plus storytelling at the Philadelphia Zoo a number of years ago, and more recently, we've received grants from the Pennsylvania Council on the Arts for Treehouse theater and an artist-in-residence. You may find that your proposal for theater requires additional explanation and clarification if you work in a zoo or aquarium—our first attempt at seeking arts funding was rejected since we weren't a traditional "theater," but a more thorough explanation, plus photos and a site visit convinced the funding agency that we did, indeed, offer a theater program.

Grants in Philadelphia and elsewhere have funded special programs for children with disabilities, disadvantaged youth, college interns, or other specific audiences. These initiatives are most often limited in time and scope, and serve best to introduce new audiences to programs, create new programs which will then be sustained through other means, or produce a one-time show, as for an exhibit opening.

We used a grant-funded pilot program to test the waters for in-zoo theater, gauge audience response, and develop a staffing plan for a long-term in-zoo program. Through evaluation, we demonstrated that our productions were educationally effective and entertaining, and that zoo visitors were eager for more shows. Wildlife Theater became a permanent seasonal offering, staffed by Treehouse Troupe actors, supplemented by interns. The additional fee-based programs we were offering in the Treehouse, which contributed to the zoo's bottom line, helped the transition from "soft money" to operating budget. By carefully managing our labor budget and conducting programs in what had traditionally been "downtime" for the building and staff, we demonstrated that educational theater could be cost-effective as well as educationally effective.

CORPORATE SPONSORSHIPS—A MOST FORTUNATE OPPORTUNITY!

Theaters and theater programs offer sponsorship and "naming" opportunities—if your audience is large enough and if your marketing/development office can negotiate the deal. Most sponsorships, by definition, provide financial support for a project or program, requiring in return that the program be named for the corporation, for example, Museum Cola Theater, or that their contribution be otherwise prominently recognized, for example, "brought to you by Museum Cola." Another important feature of such arrangements is the exchange of goods or services with the corporation—they may receive passes or museum parties as part of the sponsorship agreement. In turn, you stand to receive financial support, outreach vehicles, advertising time, in-kind services, and other goodies. Corporations, unlike most foundations, are interested in exposure, and often require their corporate name and logo to be prominently displayed on all printed materials, banners, and outreach vehicles. Sponsorships can be the source of sizable long-term financial support if the match is a good one. Be warned, though, that you may face internal competition for sponsorship dollars with exhibits, IMAX theaters, 10K runs, holiday festivals, and many other causes, and that nurturing potential sponsors is a long, arduous task requiring skill and experience—unless you get lucky.

Hint: Schmooze. Talk up your theater program, even when you're not looking for grants. You never know when the head of a foundation—even a science or research foundation—is a theater buff or an amateur actor.

Hint: Develop a network in theater circles. Be active in the theatrical community. Go to workshops, hold auditions, subscribe to journals.

DEVELOPING THE BUDGET

Developing your budget is only slightly easier than finding the money to fund it. Your program, tempered by reality, should be the jumping-off point for writing your budget. Our program started small, with just the staff and materials needed to operate Treehouse and do performances and classes for casual visitors and school classes. After we gained a firm footing, we developed fee-based programs that would bring in revenue, made projections for income and expenses, and presented a budget proposal at zoo budgeting time. I'll go into more detail later about our program and how we budget, but let's take a look at programming now.

Before you begin budgeting ask yourself a few questions. Our questions were as follows:

- Are we planning a seasonal show, a one-time exhibit or project-based performance, or will theater be an ongoing method of interpretation?

- What can our operating budget handle? (In other words, how bold or confident are we to walk into our president's office to ask for the money we need?)

- What is our vision? Can we sell it to the board? How can we make the program strong enough to become a win-win program from both budgeting and program-

matic perspectives?

At the Philadelphia Zoo, we determined that theater would be our main form of interpretation at the Treehouse, with performances held every hour throughout the day and special presentations for other programs such as overnights and birthday parties. Since theater is the backbone of our Treehouse program, we felt it was important to use full-time, salaried actors funded from the zoo's operating budget. Making the case for full-time salaried actors wasn't easy—we were one of the first, if not the first, zoo to have an acting troupe (started in 1987)—and our approach was very different from other education programs in zoos at that time. We used scripts, props, costumes, and music, but no live animals. We hired actors, not biology teachers or environmental educators.

Our first shows were presented to casual visitors and reserved school classes. Casual visitors to the Treehouse were families whose children played at hatching from giant eggs or metamorphosing into monarch butterflies as they explored the building's habitats. Schools could reserve a special orientation to the Treehouse for a more structured learning experience. For much of the year, shows were presented for three to four classes in the morning, then hourly for family visitors for the rest of the day. Because we knew that eventually we would need to rely on more internal operating revenue than grant support, we were eager to attract new visitors to Treehouse in order to raise revenue for programs and exhibit improvements. Consequently, we looked for ways to use the building (our expensive "stage set") in "down time."

Our building was nearly empty in the evening and late fall and winter afternoons. Our normal busy hours tended to occur when school groups reserved lessons in the morning hours from October through June, and during the typical summertime early afternoon and weekend crunch. So we focused our efforts on building programs around our downtime hours. The answer? Educational themed birthday parties and overnight programs.

Birthday parties were designed around an educational theme. For example, we developed and presented themed shows about butterflies or dinosaurs for birthday guests. Games, exploration time, party favors, and refreshments are traditional party accompaniments. Fees charged for parties more than cover the cost of producing them, and the revenue helps support non-fee-based activities. Last year educational parties for children at the Philadelphia Zoo had gross revenues of more than $80,000.

Overnight programs were scheduled for two nights each weekend during the school year. Our program was modeled after other museums' very successful camp-in programs. Again, theater is the primary focus of the evening program, along with games, zoo tours, and other activities. In 1999, Philadelphia Zoo NightFlights earned more than $250,000.

As we expanded our programs to increase our educational impact, we increased staff and budget. Our rule of thumb was that all programs had to be self-sustaining or grant-funded, and that theater programs would operate overall on a break-even basis. We crafted revenue margins almost as carefully as scripts, although always safeguarding our educational mission. Our theater program grew out of Treehouse and into the rest of the zoo, in the form of Wildlife Theater summer performances and ZooTales short pieces.

Our theater troupe budget grew to reflect expenses needed to operate these varied programs and our revenue grew accordingly. Our basic costs included actors' salaries (full-time staff) and benefits, substitutes and part-time staff such as stage managers/operations assistants, audio equipment, props, costumes, facility repair and enhancement (the building was our giant stage set), and program-specific expenses such as party invitations, favors, refreshments, and security and maintenance staff. Since we write most of our own scripts, fees for scriptwriting or scripts are not usually part of our budget, but this may be an important category for your institution.

Our greatest challenge came in converting our cast of part-time actors to full-time, benefited staff. Our success resulted from demonstrating a stable, cost-effective program that operated seven days a week, year round. Program

growth dictated full-time staff, not part-time or seasonal workers.

As you develop your operating budget, make sure you include the relevant categories. Your individual program may include additional expenses, but the following items constitute basic expenses:

- **Salaries** (salaries should reflect local standards; at the Philadelphia Zoo, actors' salaries approximately equal our instructors' pay scale
- **Substitute performers**
- **Audio** (don't skimp here; a decent system including cordless mics, speakers, amplifier, tape deck that will serve about 100 people or so may cost $6,000-$8,000 or more)
- **Props** (very variable depending on script, staging, etc.)
- **Costumes** (also varies greatly depending on script; hats, shirts, props, etc. may suggest costumes in lieu of full costumes)
- **Legal fees** (if you need advice on intellectual property issues)
- Music (it's possible to obtain copyright-free music, but be sure to obtain the rights if you need to)
- **Scripts** (if you don't write your own, expect to pay about $300-600 for a script from a non-profit like a museum or zoo)
- **Scenery** (varies from a simple backdrop to elaborate sets; costs vary widely for painting)
- **Publicity** (if you must buy advertising or produce publicity materials, check with your marketing department for costs and help)
- **Printing** (for collateral materials, programs, etc.)

CONCLUSION

And so, to summarize briefly the types of funding options available:

- **Foundation grants**: generally will only support a program for the first few years; can be competitive, but local foundations are good bets for support.
- **Corporate sponsorships**: a wonderful way to go!; usually require the corporation's name on all printed materials and signs. Some demand logos, specific language, and a certain size sign or banner; can offer long-term support.

- **Museum operating budget**: Generally once you get past the initial phase of starting up your program, expenses like actors' salaries should be included in your institution's operating budget; May be a hard sell initially, but program profits or good press can make an impact. Incorporate theater into fee-based programs, evaluate and disseminate your results.

Effective museum theater is possible on a shoestring or with a six-figure budget. Philadelphia Zoo programs and many others started very small but have grown rapidly--encouraged by the passion, support and guidance of individuals who believed in the power of performance. All of us in museum theater owe a debt of gratitude to former Treehouse Directors Rosemary Harms and the late Stephen Diamond, who nurtured Treehouse theater in its early days and helped create the strong artistic program that survives today.

RESPONSE TO *Budgeting for Theater*

TESSA BRIDAL
DIRECTOR OF PUBLIC PROGRAMS, SCIENCE MUSEUM OF MINNESOTA

Kathy Wagner has thoroughly outlined the basic options available to museum theater practitioners. Like the Philadelphia Zoo, the Science Museum of Minnesota has explored foundations, corporate support, and a variety of grants from federal, state, and local agencies, with varying degrees of success with all of them. I will only add a few notes of either clarification or personal insight that might prove useful to those who are new to this field.

Asking the question "Why do we want to use theater?" may seem very basic and perhaps out of place in an article on budgeting and funding. Having a clear answer to this question will nevertheless determine many of your choices and your costs. There are no wrong answers to this question. As you explore answers and define your wishes and your needs, you will be advancing your program on every level, including where to go for funds and how to approach the funders. How you answer this question will also help you discuss your ideas with colleagues, management, and boards of directors.

Anything you can do to obtain a base of operating budget support will pay off handsomely in the long run, when "soft" money (grants, etc.) either dries up or ends due to the time constraints of the source. I encourage you to base your program plans on this operating support and build from there to temporary or seasonal programs.

I also recommend establishing a strong relationship between your theater program and those planning exhibits, either permanent or temporary. Federal funders, particularly, look kindly on programs designed to enhance an exhibit experience, and it is often easier to piggy-back a theater program on an existing exhibition than it is to seek independent funding for it.

It is also well worth examining the funding available for museums, zoos, and aquariums who are partnering with schools. The American Association of Museums (AAM) is an excellent source of information for available federal funds, and your local education resources can do the same for you on a state or county basis.

In her article, Wagner mentions corporate sponsorships. SMM has been fortunate in obtaining these, some on an ongoing basis, to cover the costs of materials and operating support for a program. We have not found corporations unreasonable in their demands for recognition, often being very happy with a plaque acknowledging their support and mention of their sponsorship in printed materials. As Wagner points out, nurturing these relationships is essential to their success. Wagner mentions that if "your museum's development staff can't help you, you can still pursue grants on your own." I will only add, *with the full knowledge and support of your development staff.* It is important for them to be aware of your pursuits and for you to understand that development staffs may occasionally have good reason for asking you not to appeal to certain funders.

Community partnerships can also prove beneficial in more ways than one. SMM has recently partnered with the Minnesota Orchestra to obtain funds for a series of programs based on sound. The orchestra's contribution is to the musical segments, including the development of a sound piece to be performed by them based on sounds collected by 5th and 6th grade children and orchestrated by Libby Larson, a Minnesota composer. The museum's contribution is to develop programs based on the physics of sound and provide the playwright and actors who will work with the children on developing a script. Funding for this collaboration was obtained from the National Endowment for the Arts.

My final comments are reserved for the basic expenses.

I recommend basing salaries for theater programs on your community. There will clearly be a wide range of pay scales across the country. Many theaters—professional, educational, and community—are willing to share their pay scales with you. By calling the theaters in your area, you will receive the scale paid to union (Actors Equity) actors, and that paid to non-union actors and other theater professionals. You will then typically have a wide range of pay scales to choose from and can balance your community's values and your institution's. This will help you determine hourly, seasonal, and full-time pay and benefits.

Please keep in mind that you are not approaching these issues alone. Publications such as this one are designed to help and support you, and there are more of them. When I took over SMM's theater program and offered the first Theater Workshop, there were no institutions I could invite to present their work at it. Now, at least three guest presenters, often including the Philadelphia Zoo, attend the workshop each year to share their experiences and their work. Resource centers containing articles, evaluations, and the names of others working in this field exist in at least three sites. Museum theater professionals are generous in sharing their expertise and their support. Don't hesitate to call upon us, we're there to help you!

CHAPTER 8

PUPPETRY

Kevin Frisch

WHY USE PUPPETS?

Everyone loves a good puppet show. Puppets are a familiar part of people's lives all around the world. Puppets are on television and used extensively in film productions. They are found in street corner performances, in shopping malls, libraries, and even Broadway shows. Schools and zoos have discovered the educational value of puppet shows, while children's hospitals use puppets to explain medical procedures in a nonthreatening way to children who must undergo certain treatments. Puppets are also used as therapeutic tools. In some cases a person who may not be at ease expressing himself will find it easier to communicate his feelings through a puppet.

Puppets represent a kind of magic and fantasy to children and nostalgia for adults, recalling happy childhood memories. The fact that puppets can entertain and make people laugh is no secret. What some may not realize is that for as long as puppets have been entertaining, they have also been educating. Puppets have been casting their spell on audiences since ancient times. People around the world have used puppets in religious ceremonies or to pass on stories of previous generations. Puppets have been found in the tombs of ancient Egypt. Aristotle and Archemedes mention the use of puppets in ancient Greece to tell the stories of the *Iliad* and the *Odyssey*. The Catholic Church used puppets to tell biblical stories to the early Christians, many of whom were illiterate. The term "marionette" (string puppet) was coined from these shows, meaning "little Mary," referring to the Virgin Mary. Even operas have been written for marionettes.

Today, puppetry is in full swing. The amount of educational programming that is available on television is overwhelming. Why are puppets so successful as educators? The secret of their success is really no secret at all—*puppets make learning fun*! A child could learn about the living habits of an animal from a book or lecture, but what if the animal could show and tell the child himself!

However, puppetry is one of the most complex theater forms and, as such, presents many challenges. Yet, I believe it to be one of the best ways to communicate ideas.

It can take years to become truly fluent with this medium. While an entire book could be written on techniques for building and manipulating puppets, my goal here is simply to offer some guidance from my own experiences to those who wish to incorporate puppetry into their programs. The following are some of what I consider to be the most important elements in creating a successful puppet show.

I have been building and performing puppet shows professionally since 1986. That was the year I began working with a permanent marionette theater located in Brooklyn, New York, The PUPPETWORKS Incorporated. There I performed six days a week, two and sometimes three shows a day for nine years. In 1995, I moved back to my hometown of Cincinnati, Ohio, and opened the Frisch Marionette Company. I occasionally build puppets for collectors, television or magazine ads, and since 1994, have designed and built hand puppets, masks, and full-body costumes for the Central Park Wildlife Center in New York City. Puppetry is a perfect combination of everything I love (art, drama, and music) and it allows me to see a vision through from beginning to end, concept to performance without compromise.

BUILDING A PUPPET SHOW

TYPES OF PUPPETS

There are many kinds of puppets; hand puppets, rod puppets, mouth and rod puppets, marionettes (string puppets), and shadow puppets. Your performance space will help determine which type of puppet you choose. Here are some questions you might ask yourself.

- Will the show be performed indoors or outdoors?
- Will the puppets be handling props?

- What level of expertise do your performers have in the field of puppetry?
- Is there going to be interaction between live actors and the puppets?
- Is your stage stationary?
- How much set-up time do you need?
- Is your stage elevated?

HAND PUPPETS

Note that there are two types of hand puppets:

The *Glove Puppet*—the puppeteer's thumb and middle finger fit into the arms of the puppet and the index finger fits into its head. (The size of the glove puppet is restricted by the proportions of the puppeteer's hand.)

The *Mouth Puppet*—the puppeteer's thumb fits into the lower jaw of the puppet and the other four fingers work the upper jaw to open and close the mouth.

Hand puppets are probably the most familiar type of puppet and most commonly used.

- They are easy to manipulate.
- They are easily packed, unpacked, and stored
- Hand puppets are naturally elevated because the puppeteer operates them from below the stage (inside a booth or behind a screen).
- The hand puppet show adapts well to outdoor settings.
- The hand puppet booth can be made of a series of canvas flats, pin-hinged together.
- The booth can be put together in minutes and easily transported from location to location.
- They handle props easily.

Here are some basics in operating a mouth puppet (hand puppet with a working mouth). The puppeteer's thumb works the chin or lower jaw and the fingers work the upper. To make the puppet's speech believable, the lower jaw should move more than the upper. This is the way humans speak. Have the puppeteers look in the mirror and try to copy their own mouth movements. The puppet's mouth opens on the syllable or vocal impulse and not between. This may sound obvious, but there are a few people who will need a little extra practice to master this bit of coordination.

ROD PUPPETS

Rod puppets are similar to glove puppets in that they are operated from below. Rather than the puppeteer's index finger inside the head, a main support rod that is secured to the puppet's head and passes through the puppet's body is held in one hand while two rods attached to each arm are held in the other.

- Movements are more restricted than that of a hand puppet or marionette.
- They are easily packed and unpacked for quick set-ups.
- Rod puppets are naturally elevated because the puppeteer operates them from below the stage (inside the booth).
- The rod puppet show plays well in outdoor settings.
- The rod puppet booth can be made of a series of canvas flats, pin-hinged together.
- The booth can be put together in minutes and easily transported from location to location.
- It does not handle props as well as hand puppets (often props are   attached to sticks, as well)

COMBINATION MOUTH AND ROD PUPPETS

This is a mouth puppet with arms (operated by rods) attached to its sides.

- Very expressive
- They can be made very large for easy visibility by the audience.

SHADOW PUPPETS

Shadow puppets are typically flat jointed figures controlled from behind or below, against a translucent screen. A single light source shines on the screen from behind. As the puppets are moved against the screen, only their black silhouette or shadows can be seen by the audience. Chinese and Indonesian shadow puppets are made from animal skins treated until they are very translucent. The skins are cut into the appropriate puppet shapes; then patterns or designs are cut and the puppet is painted with transparent dyes to add color to the images. These are very beautiful and elaborate puppets, but a simple shadow puppet can be made from cardboard cut-outs.

Color can be added to the puppet by cutting details out of the figure and covering the open spaces with gels or cellophane paper.

The joints of the figure can be joined with paper fasteners or string running through the two pieces and knotted on each end.

The control rods can be made from hanger wire straightened and looped at one end. The looped end is tied onto the puppet with string.

The puppets and the screen are flat so they can be easily stored when not in use.

The screen is made from a simple wooden frame (generally wider than it is high) on which translucent material is stretched. Suggestion: tightly woven muslin or sports nylon.

MARIONETTES

Marionettes are puppets that are worked by strings from above the stage. Traditionally, they are wooden figures from 15 to 30 inches in height. This is the size range of my marionettes, which can be seen comfortably by an audience of 350-400 children. Puppets that are larger than this should be made of lighter materials such as foam rubber, Styrofoam, or cardboard shapes, aluminum, or cloth.

Learning to control a marionette takes a great deal of time and is a bit like learning to play a musical instrument. The puppeteer does not have direct contact with the puppet. The size and weight of the puppet have great bearing on how the puppet will behave. The advantages of marionettes are numerous and the challenges great.

- The full figure of the puppet is visible, which adds tremendously to the illusion of autonomous movement
- A marionette can mimic every human movement and can also do things humans can't— fly, split apart, and rejoin; they can run, jump, and dance convincingly.
- Marionette stages consist of the stage and a bridge, on which the performers stand.
- The puppets are operated from above the stage.
- If performing for large audiences, the stage should be elevated for clear visibility.
- Marionettes are probably the most difficult to make and control.
- The skill needed to work a marionette comes from experience.

- There are many types of marionette controls: horizontal, vertical, paddle, and variations of each. The way in which the puppet is manipulated can be very different for each of these controls, too numerous to mention here. However there are basic skills that every marionettist must learn—keeping the puppet in a stance without sagging on the stage or *floating* off of it; walking the puppet; focusing the puppet on the action; and gesturing.

DEVELOPMENT

SCRIPT

Audience sensibilities change with the times, so it is important to always be aware of what is acceptable at the time of the performance while maintaining the integrity of your work. Remember that you are writing for children or young adults. The children will often be with their parents, so avoid off-color humor. Put your audience at ease without any fear of embarrassment. Children often want to imitate the characters they see. This can be put to effective use in educational programming, but it can also be a nightmare for parents if the child is imitating bad behavior.

Many elements go into making a great puppet show. The puppet show, like other theater pieces, will only be as good as the script. The script is the foundation upon which everything else rests. Even when a performance is improvisational, it must have a structure. This means that the performers must have a thorough knowledge of their craft and how to work an audience. I would not suggest improvisation unless your performers are experienced and adept at manipulating puppets.

As for scripting puppet theater, when writing a script for puppets always keep in mind the characteristics that make puppets unique to theater. Remember that a puppet is not alive. The puppeteer's goal is to create the illusion of life. Therefore, the puppets must move with deliberate actions, actions that appear to have thought behind them. The audience should be able to "see" the puppets "think." This is why I say deliberate action.

Remember, it's a puppet-show, not a radio-play. This may seem rudimentary to some, but I have seen countless puppet shows where the puppets enter the stage and proceed to deliver pun after pun and one-liners. Now puns and one-liners have their place, but don't burden your script with them.

Avoid long speeches. Another mistake that writers sometimes make is to stress a point or teach a lesson by turning out a long speech. Nothing will put an audience to sleep faster than a lecturing puppet. The puppets are actors, not props. Puppets can do incredible things. Exploit this fact in your script. For example, puppets are notorious for slapstick humor (physical comedy). I believe the term "slapstick" was made popular by Mr. Punch's use of his slapstick in Punch and Judy puppet shows. A word of warning about getting too physical: today's audiences enjoy slapstick humor but have very low tolerance for violence. Audiences (or parents) seem to make a distinction between violence in cartoons and violence in puppet shows. Perhaps it is because puppets are three-dimensional and therefore more "real." What may play well in a cartoon might not go over as well in a puppet show.

CHARACTER

This brings us to characterization. My advice is to keep it simple. Puppets are fantastic at being one dimensional—good, bad, evil, sneaky, silly, and so on. Your audience easily understands the character's motive. This may even solicit reactions from the audience, cheers for the puppet of virtue, or hisses for the villain, and laughter for the clown. How then do we represent evil or bad characters without offending the audience or glamorizing the character? My method is simple, but I do have to walk a fine line. I present a character that is wicked or villainous by making their motives evil and their actions absurd (slapstick). In this way, the character is a source of tension, but also comic relief. A word of warning: don't make the villain the source of too much laughter or the audience will hate to see it go. For instance, in my production of Hansel & Gretel, Rossina Sweettooth (the witch) loves nothing more than throwing children into the oven and baking them into gingerbread! What a horrifying prospect! However, by making all of her actions toward that goal absurd, she immediately draws laughter from the crowd the first time she enters the stage! Evil characters should be the butt of jokes and they should be made worthy of their just desserts! Children understand. At any rate that is how I handle evil characters by making them buffoons.

Avoid street talk. It is my opinion that phrases like "you're stupid," "shut-up," or how about this all-time favorite "Shut-up stupid," have no place in children's programming. First of all, it shows a lack of creativity on the part of the writer and even more important, these are the types of phrases that children inevitably latch onto and repeat for weeks on end ad nauseam. A parent accompanying a child to your performance might be hesitant to return for fear of what other "cute" habits the child might learn from you.

MUSIC

I use music in all of my shows. An overture helps to settle an audience and at the same time creates anticipation for what they are about to see.

- Music can set the pace of the show.
- Music between scenes can help make a transition in the tone or mood of the audience.
- Music can reinforce the emotions of a character when played under the dialogue.
- Giving a character a song to sing can break up the dialogue and can give great insight to a character.
- Songs are great when they help the plot along.

For instance, in my production of *The Wizard of Oz*, the music traces America's musical heritage from the spirituals of home to jazz in the Emerald City. The Strawman, Lion, and Tinman all sing the blues. As for the Wicked Witch of the West, I made her crazy and colorful with the personality of a tightly wound rubber band, so of course she's got to 'scat' in 1920s jazz style while flying on a broomstick!

I know that many puppeteers lift songs and music directly from sound recordings and that is fine if they have the permission to do so. But beware of copyrights! If there is a piece of music you want to use, you have to contact the owner of the copyright. If you don't know who that is, call ASCAP (1-800-99-ASCAP) to get pointed in the right direction. The music you want to use may be public domain, but if it is not and you use it, that is tantamount to stealing. A better way to go is to audition young composers and have original music written for your program. You might even decide to make your own compact discs or tape cassettes, so that your audience can take a piece of the show home with them! And who knows, you might help launch the career of the next Sondhiem! Fortunately, I have access to a wonderful musician and composer, my brother Steve Frisch.

PUPPETS—STORE-BOUGHT OR CUSTOM-MADE?

Once the script is written it will serve as a road map for the actual construction of the show. The show consists of puppets, props, sets, and a stage. Custom-made puppets are always better than off-the-shelf or store-bought puppets for public performances.

- Store-bought puppets are usually toys and not intended to be put through the rigors of professional use.
- They are often made to fit the hands of a child.
- They also tend to look stale and generic.

Custom-made puppets are more expensive but:

- They can be made to precisely suit your needs.
- A well-made custom puppet gives the show the look of professionalism.
- They will withstand daily use (if properly made) and can be retouched and refurbished over time.
- A hand-made puppet also has a uniqueness that the audience perceives and appreciates.

However, if your budget is tight and by some miracle a store happens to have a puppet that fits the bill, then, by all means, use it.

It is possible to put on a show with store-bought puppets, but in my opinion, if something is worth doing, then do it well. In my own shows I spend a great deal of time carving, sculpting, and painting individual characters which ensures that my shows are unique and exactly as I envisioned them. Give your shows the best possible chance of success.

TO USE OR NOT TO USE . . . PROPS.

In my own marionette productions, I use props and set-pieces. For puppet shows in general, I believe that props help to create the illusion of life and illustrate the points being made. Some exceptions to the use of props are improvisational pieces and dance works, but the goals are completely different. It would be impossible to have every prop that may be needed in an improvisation. Also, the

live-performers' actions, such as driving a car or sipping tea, are readily recognizable by the audience. The actor relies heavily on pantomime and facial expression.

In a puppet show, puppets try to attain basic human movements in order to be believable. Props and set pieces are an important part of the puppet's "world." The props actually help to attain that believability. It takes the guess work out of the equation on the part of the audience. In short, if a prop will help illustrate a point, it makes sense to use it.

PROPS, SIMPLE OR ELABORATE?

Do props need to be elaborate? Not necessarily. They only need to be easily recognizable by the audience. They can be beautiful illustrations painted on plywood cutouts, or you might find miniature replicas of what you need (like pots, pans, baskets, phones, watering cans, etc.) in craft shops and toy stores. I carve small props from wood and larger props can be made from Styrofoam shapes covered with glue-soaked paper mache, cheesecloth, or felt. The methods for making props are as varied as the props themselves. The possibilities are too numerous to mention here, but if you and your staff are interested in making props yourselves, please look at the reference list included with this chapter.

THE BASICS OF MANIPULATION

It can take years for puppeteers to truly be proficient at their craft and, needless to say, the amount of time we have for perfection is severely limited. With this in mind, the ultimate goal will be to get the director's vision of the script onto the stage. It is possible with good direction in a limited amount of time to get a good show from inexperienced puppeteers. The type of person I look for to become a puppeteer is someone who is artistic, has had some acting experience, has a good understanding of human behavior, and can take direction well.

FOCUS

Once the performers are assembled they will need some time to become acquainted with the puppets. Start with the basics. Before rehearsals start, teach movements you know they will be using in the show. First is how to focus the puppet. Focus is the key to believable interaction. By focus I mean have the puppet follow the action with its eyes or look at who it's talking to. Pretend to look at different members of the audience. The worst thing that a puppet can do is to stare into space with it's mouth open (unless it is supposed to look like a zombie!). Remember, the goal is to create the illusion of life. Always keep in mind how the audience is seeing the puppet and where the eyes of the puppet are focused.

ACTIONS SPEAK LOUDER THAN WORDS

Unlike a human actor, the puppet needs deliberate movement when it is speaking or it appears lifeless. Emphasize important words. When the puppet is not speaking it should have minimal or no movement (except for appropriate reactions) to avoid upstaging the puppet that is speaking. Simply moving the puppet is not enough. An amateur's nervous jiggling of a puppet is the equivalent of gibberish speech. It is unintelligible. The puppet's movements should be broad and well defined. Pantomime the dialogue. If the sound were turned off, the audience should still have a good idea of what the puppet is trying to communicate. In a puppet show, action is the name of the game. Give your audience something to look at. Illustrating an action is far more entertaining than simply talking about it. When the audience is preoccupied with the action of the puppet rather than the puppet itself, viewers begin to suspend their disbelief.

- The puppet's movements should always complement the speech or action of the play. The puppet should have some action to complete on each of its lines.

- The puppet should nod in the affirmative when speaking a positive and shake its head when disagreeing or speaking a negative.

- If the puppet is referring to a prop, point to it! Walk to it! Pick it up! Don't let there be any mistake as to what "it" is that the puppet is talking about!

STAGING AND DIRECTING THE SHOW

Once the puppeteer has a decent working vocabulary of movements, it's time to block the show. This means positioning and choreographing the general movement of the show (where the puppets are on the stage in relation to each other).

- Blocking should be done line by line, one scene at a time. At this point I want little or no puppetry happening on stage. I run the scene without any actual acting from the puppets. This ensures that the new puppeteer is not overwhelmed and is able to memorize the order of the show.

- After the initial blocking is done, I start from the beginning and add movement to the puppets, giving each puppeteer specific actions for each line. This can be painstaking, but it actually saves time in the long run. A live actor doesn't need to be shown how to walk from here to there, but an amateur puppeteer must be shown how to make the puppet look as if it is walking from point to point. At this stage, any puppetry that is happening is being learned by rote. The key here is that by rehearsing in this way the puppeteer is building a vast library of movements that can be used spontaneously when the puppeteer has become an expert.

- The scene is then run several times, with each run-through adding more and more specific and detailed movements. As your puppeteers digest each new bit of information, you can parcel out more information until they have sufficiently mastered all the movements they will need for the show. I rehearse each scene and act this way until finally the entire show has been staged. By now working a puppet is becoming second nature to your staff. Your puppeteers are more comfortable and starting to really interact with each other. But, don't stop there.

- Videotape your show from start to finish. Sit down with the cast and review their performances and give them notes. This will be the first time they have seen the show from the audience's perspective, which can be an invaluable tool for training your staff and perfecting the show.

- Take a break, then with "fresh eyes" watch the video without the cast present. Try to view it as if it were the first time you have seen the show. Are you amused or entertained by what you see? If not, more work needs to be done. If you are a person who is easily amused, find someone who is not and have them watch. Are there weak spots in the show?

- Rehearse again, tweaking and strengthening the weak moments.

- Consider inviting a group or two to watch dress rehearsals and take note of the audience reactions.

- Give comment forms to teachers and invite children to write letters to your group.

CONCLUSION

In conclusion, you will know if your show is successful if it commands the audience's attention and if they react at the appropriate moments and in the appropriate manner.

- Keep the show moving! Don't give the audience an opportunity to be distracted. This is especially important with outdoor performances where the environmental distractions are numerous.

- Do not begrudge the audience if they aren't reacting the way you might like them to. I assure you it is not their fault!

- Different children react differently. Allow them to react in the way that is most comfortable for them. Some children may be wary and afraid of the puppet or costumed character, so do not force the puppet on them. In most instances, they are as curious about the puppet as they are unsure of it and are quite content to watch from a "safe" distance.

The challenges of puppetry are many and ongoing, but the rewards are even greater. Puppetry can have a profound impact on a child's life and create wonderful memories that can last a lifetime. Performing a puppet for a child and seeing the expression of wonder and delight on his or her face can be very addictive. So be warned, if you decide to incorporate puppets into your program, you might just end up making it your career as I have!

If you accept the challenges of entertaining and teaching the world with puppets then I encourage you to join one or both of these organizations:

The Puppeteers of America
Membership office #5 Cricklewood Path
Pasadena, California 91107-1002

UNIMA-USA
1404 Spring St. NW
Atlanta, Georgia 30309

I have also compiled a brief list of reference materials which have been very helpful to me:
  The Art of the Puppet by Bil Baird
  Puppets-Methods and Materials by Cedric Flower & Alan Fortney
  Making Puppets Come Alive by Larry Engler and Carol Fijan

The Prop Builder's Mask-Making Handbook, by Thurston James
Shadow Puppets by Olive Blackham
Puppetry Today by Helen Binyon
Marionettes: A Hobby for Everyone by Mabel and Les Beaton
Rod, Shadow and Glove Puppets from the Little Angel Theater by John Wright

- Connect to: The Puppetry Homepage
    http://www.sagecraft.com/puppetry

- Contact Kevin Frisch at:
    5901 Hickoryknoll Drive
    Cincinnati, Ohio 45233
    Phone: (513) 451-8875

RESPONSE TO *Puppetry*

ROBERT A. FINTON
SUPERVISOR OF PUBLIC PROGRAMS, MARYLAND SCIENCE CENTER

Kevin Frisch's article made me take a step back and see that puppetry is, indeed, a wonderful entertainment tool that can educate. Not only that, but it made me realize that I've been using puppets to educate without really thinking about it. These marvelous creatures of cloth and wood are often overlooked as the powerful educators that they can be. In many ways puppets can provide (in a performance, demonstration, or other educational venue) that which cannot be had financially, spatially, or stylistically. In my work at the Maryland Science Center, I've written a dinosaur program for K-3rd grade where my puppet is a life-sized, three-dimensional ornitholestes. Getting hold of a real dinosaur these days can prove extremely challenging. A puppet can also reduce the expense of casting. To date, I've yet to hear of Bert or Ernie requiring health benefits, (though their handlers might). Also, with my puppet Moses the Mouse, I've discovered he can play all the roles of an entire Cecil B. De Mille feature right on my lap. The need for extended staging has thus far been held to a minimum.

Keep in mind, one need not incorporate puppets solely into puppet shows. Most of my work with puppets has been to incorporate them into a live presentation or lesson. Fortunately, puppets tend to be very willing co-stars and can even be used as the focal point of the educational theme. A most interesting feature I learned about puppetry is that when it is done well one really doesn't need flats or curtains to hide the puppeteer. One of my most vivid puppet memories is of watching Johnny Carson talk with Kermit the Frog while ignoring Jim Henson. And Henson was not a ventriloquist! The other nice aspect about using puppets to educate is they can be the ones to ask the intimidating (stupid) questions, and children are always smarter than the puppet.

When including puppetry into educational presentations, Kevin is correct with regard to the initial expense of a puppet (whether financially or with blood, sweat, and tears). One needs a puppet to be durable, fitted to the puppeteer, and worthy of the show. When taken on with proper planning and some good support, puppets are a unique and exotic addition to any performance. But, overall, they are just pure fun anyway it goes.

CHAPTER 9

MUSEUM THEATER AND TECHNOLOGY

Mike Alexander, Manager of Public Programs and Science Theater
Museum of Science, Boston

Enter *Leonardo.*

At times, *Leonardo* seemed larger than life. In early 1996, the Museum of Science in Boston decided to present an exhibition on the life, science, and art of Leonardo da Vinci. The amount of information we wanted to get across was overwhelming and contradictory. The problems often seemed unresolvable. The sheer size of the exhibit was larger than the space we had available. And the theater production, chosen to end the visitors' experiences, was our biggest theatrical undertaking.

As so often seems to happen with our plays, there came the time in the production stage when the playwright and director, Jon Lipsky, and I performed our ritual in which he came up with wonderful ideas for staging while I tried to keep him connected to reality. I remember sitting in an almost dark, far-from-finished theater space just a few days before the opening of the exhibit to which Boston's elite had been invited. Jon had just had another idea, one that would add significantly to the production values of the play, and one that, surprisingly enough, I could do without too much work using our computerized lighting and sound system. I told him we could do what he wanted, but there was something he should know: If I did it, he would have reached a new benchmark in our productions. The computer's capacity would be completely used up.

When the Museum of Science began using theater as an educational tool in the 1980s, we decided to try to include production values that would be comparable to those used in more standard theaters. We felt that professional playwrights, directors, composers, and, of course, actors, were essential to make the program successful. To these, we wanted to add theatrical lighting, sound, sets, and properties. While these goals seemed worthy, the reality was that our budget would not support all these professionals and a person to control lighting and sound during each performance. Something had to give.

Eventually, we came up with the scheme of having the actors themselves control the lighting and sound cues by means of a small remote control unit that they would carry with them. The remote control would cause a computer to perform a programmed action such as fading up a stage light. This was, to us, an ideal solution. It solved the budget problem; it added to the overall magic of the performance as visitors tried to figure out how these things were happening right on cue; and, perhaps most significantly, it gave us an excuse to have some fun playing around with technology.

Before I go any farther, let me say I am a big supporter of theater as an educational tool. I believe that theater is often the best way to get across a point or to engage visitors or to ensure that a concept will be remembered. In other museums, as well as in Boston, I have seen actors on the floor with nothing more than their acting skills doing remarkable jobs educating. In this chapter, I am not at all saying technology is necessary for a successful theater production, only that the means exist to add, without a great deal of time or expense, virtually any dramatic effect you desire. Even just a few years ago, a certain amount of technical expertise was needed to do these things, but, as in so many other areas of life, the digital revolution has changed all the rules.

I will begin by covering a few broad areas of theatrical technology and how they can be added in stages as funds become available and then get into methods of integrating these into a completely computer-controlled system that is limited only by your imagination. As I go along, I will give examples from our plays here in Boston, show how *Leonardo* challenged our first system, and how we have significantly expanded our capabilities with an off-the-shelf wonder called Trax.

LIGHTING

Probably no single addition to a theater production will have as much impact as good lighting. Not all white light is white. If you have ever taken a picture indoors using outdoor film, you know how yellow and anemic looking the resulting picture is. Our senses fool us into thinking indoor lighting is making light of the same color as natural sunlight. It takes something as unbiased as a camera to show us reality. Theatrical lighting comes in a number of color temperatures. Generally speaking, the higher the color temperature, the more natural the light.

Several years ago, the Museum of Science presented a short play in a exhibition about gems. The play was produced at a time when we had very little money available to us and we were forced to use the regular track-light fixtures that are used for all our exhibits. The actor wore a beautiful blue and yellow velvet robe but the track lighting washed out the colors until they looked very ordinary. We used the same robe in another program on a stage that had theatrical lighting. What a difference! The colors really popped out at you. Unfortunately, because our senses deceive us, the best way to see the difference is to set up a test where regular indoor lighting can be alternated with stage lighting. Try it some time; I guarantee you will never want to use regular lighting again.

Theatrical lights also have other advantages. They are usually much brighter; they can be tinted with colored gels; they can be tightly focused so that they light only what you want lit; and, if you can afford a dimming system, the brightness of the lights can be varied. This last aspect is very useful in plays. It is easy to change the mood or setting of a play by changing the light level.

We are currently doing a play about heart transplants. In it, a committee must decide which of several potential recipients will receive the next available heart. This decision is made several months before a heart actually became available after a fatal accident, but the audience was misunderstanding, thinking instead that this decision was made at the same time as the accident. This was considered an important point to make by our advisors. Changing the dialogue did not emphasize the point sufficiently, nor did the movements of the actors. A simple light change at this point of the play cleared up the confusion.

Dimming systems have become very sophisticated over the last several years. When I first became involved with theater, the dimmers were large, expensive, and controlled by individual analog channels from a light board. Since we could only afford a few dimmers, an elaborate "patch panel" was needed to connect a specific group of lights to a dimmer. When the level of the control channel was raised, all the lights responded together. Now, most dimming systems are small, less expensive, and digital. The normal practice in theaters is to connect a single light to a dimmer. This means that each light can be adjusted independently or as part of a group of lights.

Of course, dimmers must be controlled by someone, either a person off stage using a light board, or, as we do, by the actors themselves using a small, radio frequency transmitter that triggers a computer. If you choose a light board, be sure it has the capacity to set up two scenes, the current scene and the next scene. Light boards with this feature will usually have what is called a "split fader" that allows one scene to be faded smoothly into the next. All the dimmer settings for the next scene may then be set while the current scene is in progress.

Dimmers, and consequently light boards, may be either analog or digital. The older analog light boards generally work by varying a control voltage from 0-10 volts DC and sending that signal to a specific dimmer. One unfortunate side effect of this is that separate wires are need for each dimmer. In large systems, this really becomes significant. The newer digital boards will send a stream of numbers over a single cable to all the dimmers. Each dimmer has its own digital address and only those targeted by the light board respond. There are several incompatible digital systems available, but if there is any standard, it is a system called DMX. If you have analog dimmers currently but want to convert to digital dimmers in the future, converters are available that will change the signal from a digital light board or computer into the signals needed by analog dimmers.

There are also computerized light boards. These are basically dedicated processors that control dimmers. They make it possible to program in as many light cues as are needed for a show and then to advance from one to the next by hitting a "go" button. Some of these boards have external inputs that can be programmed to initiate the "go" function and can, therefore, be connected to a wireless remote control button such as we use. With a little ingenuity, these light boards can be set up to activate tape decks, control volumes, or start motorized props all at the touch of the wireless remote.

MICROPHONES

A friend of mine once said to me that in order to educate, you've got to be heard. For those of us who educate in a museum, this is often a real challenge. The Museum of Science prides itself in its fun, interactive exhibits. Unfortunately for an actor, such exhibits are often loud. A quiet, out-of the way theater space may seem to be the ideal solution, but such areas are often areas where it is difficult to gather an audience. One time (and so far only one time) I was able to convince the designer of an exhibit to allow me to turn down the volume controls of the exhibits during plays on a nearby stage. Then, there are wireless microphones. I still believe that an actor sounds better without a mike, but sometimes there is no option. In a small, quiet theater I do not use mikes, but out in exhibits, where the noise level is much higher, I almost always use them. I want the actors to concentrate on their acting and educating, not on shouting.

Many companies make very good wireless microphones. The days when a program would be interrupted by a passing taxi driver giving colorful descriptions of fellow drivers are long gone. There are a few things to look for when purchasing a system. The microphone transmitters worn by actors should be easy to use and rugged. I spent thousands of dollars installing a museum-wide system of microphones from a very reputable company only to find that after a year or so of use, the covers to the battery compartments all broke off and we had to hold the batteries in the transmitters with rubber bands. The system should have many frequencies available. Even if only one or two are purchased initially, there should be room for expansion. Some companies not only offer different frequencies, but will also conduct computer searches for the best frequencies for a given situation. Is there a TV station nearby? . . . a police station (as we have right next door)? . . . an airport? . . . a taxi company? All these are powerful radio frequency sources and should be taken into account when buying a system. The world is becoming more and more dependent on radio frequencies and this situation will only get worse.

The microphone receivers installed in a sound system should be what is called diversity receivers. These receivers are actually composed of two independent receivers. An electronic switch chooses between the stronger of the two signals to prevent drop outs as actors move about the stage. Another very nice feature is an antenna distribution system. Each diversity receiver uses two antennas. If there are three or four actors in a play, it is easy to become buried in antennas. Distribution systems avoid this by using a single pair of antennas and distributing the signals to all of the receivers in a system.

Another real problem with microphone systems of all types, wired and wireless, is feedback. The whole point behind using microphones is to allow for the microphones to be relatively loud. The problem is, if an actor moves close to a speaker, a teeth-jarring whine will be caused. To some extent, this problem can be solved by the placement of the speakers used in a system. Sometimes, however, a speaker must be fairly close to the stage. I have found this to be a particular problem in small but loud areas of the museum. Another way around the problem is it use a 1/3 octave equalizer. Feedback tends to be greatest at certain sound frequencies determined by the physical dimensions of the space. Equalizers allow specific sound frequencies to be reduced. Adjusting a 1/3 octave equalizer is more an art than a science, but with a bit of experience they can be set up to eliminate practically all feedback. Within the last few years, a third solution has been developed. There is now a device called a feedback eliminator which automatically identifies and reduces frequencies that cause feedback. This is an amazing gadget that does its job superbly well. Whenever I have a particularly difficult situation where I know feedback will be a problem, I don't even try the first two methods, I just get a feedback eliminator and ten minutes later, the problem is solved.

Let me make one last point about wireless microphones. Wireless microphones use up lots of batteries. I would very much like to use rechargeable batteries but they tend to run out of charge very quickly. With a regular alkaline battery, the charge declines slowly and there is usually plenty of charge left to get through the rest of a performance. With rechargeable batteries, the first indication that they are weak is that they stop working—usually right in the middle of a show. As much as I hate to do it, and until someone builds a better battery, I recommend using disposable batteries in any performance situation.

MUSIC AND SOUND EFFECTS

Music and sound add another whole dimension to plays. Whether it is background music to emphasize the emotions of a scene, the sound effect of a passing car, music for a dance, or the accompaniment for a song, I believe music is a great way to add to the production values of a play. The equipment available makes this addition quite simple.

The easiest way to add music is with a cassette tape deck. Many manufacturers have models that will work well in this application. If it is possible to have the music controlled by a person off stage, there are really no considerations in the selection of a deck. If, however your actors are going to control the music, there are a couple of things to take into account. First, a method is needed to start the deck. This can, of course, be built into the blocking of a play. If it fits the overall style, the deck can even be right out on stage. In the gems play I mentioned earlier, the actor was a sort of "out of time" character who had lived in the past yet knew all about the present. The actor carried a boom-box and used it to play music that went along with a historical narration that took the form of a minuet. I rather liked the odd juxtaposition of history, science, dance, and the almost-jarring appearance of the boom-box.

Usually it is necessary to be more subtle when starting a tape deck. Most professional tape decks have remote controls. The only problem with these controls is that they are often either infrared or wired. Infrared controls, just like a television clicker, must be pointed at the tape deck in order for them to work. Wired controls may be positioned anywhere on stage, but if the control is moved, the wires drag along behind. Neither is subtle. At the Museum of Science, we solved this problem by modifying a slide projector remote control to suit our needs. It is a simple matter for a technician to modify the remote control receiver so that it connects to the tape deck through the deck's wired remote control input. The big advantage to this is that wireless slide projector remote controls are available that use radio waves (as opposed to infrared light). Radio waves will go in all directions through walls and clothing and so the transmitter does not have to be pointed at the

receiver. The transmitters and receivers can operate at different frequencies or can have different digital address codes that ensure that one transmitter does not interfere with another.

The actors may carry the transmitters in their pockets, and when they wish to start some music, they need only push a button. This can be done very unobtrusively. Staff members at our museum who know about, or have even used, these remote controls, have told me they can never see the actors starting the music. A visitor one time stopped me after a play and said that not only had he loved the play, but he was so impressed that the actors could time their acting to such an extent that they all started singing just when the tape deck got to the music! He imagined that the actors had started a tape at the beginning of the play, acted for ten or 15 minutes while the blank tape was running and then timed their entry to coordinate with the start of the recorded music. The magic of the theater . . . .

The other major consideration when selecting a tape deck is stopping the deck. If only one piece of music is being used, this really isn't a problem: it is only necessary to let the deck run until the end of the tape. The situation becomes more complicated if several pieces of music or sound effects are being used. The same radio frequency remote control that was used to start the deck can also be wired to stop it, but this method has two serious drawbacks. One, the actors must remember to push the button or the next piece of music will start. And two, even if the actors remember to stop it, if they do not stop it at precisely the same spot each time, it will be difficult for them to time their entry for the next piece. Even one or two seconds can seem like an eternity to a actor who has started singing only to find that the music hasn't begun.

The easiest way around this problem is to use a tape deck that has a cue track. This is generally the third or fourth track on a deck and is entirely separate from the two stereo tracks. I remember the old film strip projectors that had a recorded sound track which included a beep every time the strip was to be advanced: that's not what I am talking about. These decks allow a tone that is never heard to be recorded on the cue track which stops the deck. This means that the tape can be cued up to the same spot over and over.

SOUND MIXERS

If several sources of sound, such as microphones and tape decks, are being used, it is necessary to mix together the various sound signals into one or two channels that, in turn, are sent to an amplifier and speakers. Sound mixers are used to accomplish this. Mixers generally will have several inputs for both microphone level and tape deck or "line" level signals. Any of these inputs may be of two types: balanced and unbalanced.

Home stereos use unbalanced inputs and outputs. The sound cords used to connect one piece of a stereo to another will have the familiar connectors called RCA type connectors. Inside each sound cord is a central wire. The wire is surrounded by a second conductor, completing the electrical circuit, that shields the center wire from interference caused by other electrical devices such as motors or radio transmitters. These connectors and cords are sufficient for most installations, but sometimes problems will arise. If the interference is strong, the shielding in unbalanced cables may not be adequate. Hums in the sound system can also be caused when the "ground" or electrical reference point of one device is connected to another.

Professional sound equipment uses balanced connectors. These connectors are much larger than the RCA type and are called XLR type connectors. Inside each sound cord are the two wires necessary to complete the electrical circuit and both are surrounded by a third conductor that provides shielding. In complicated systems using lots of equipment, hums are more easily eliminated with XLR connectors. In difficult situations when there is strong interference, balanced systems often perform better than unbalanced systems. I would recommend starting out with equipment that uses balanced connectors.

Many mixers will provide both balanced and unbalanced inputs for different types of equipment. For instance, in a system I worked on recently, the microphones and video tape decks were all balanced while the CD player and computer sound card were unbalanced. For the best performance, always connect equipment to the appropriate type of input. The voltage of the electrical signals produced by balanced and unbalanced equipment is different. Transformers are available to change one type into the other if the correct inputs are not available on a mixer.

Another valuable feature of mixers is a pan or balance control for each input. In single-speaker systems this is not really an issue since all the sound ends up coming out of the same speaker. In a stereo system these controls allow the monaural signal from a microphone to be distributed equally to the two speakers without affecting the stereo signals from a tape deck. Without this feature the voice of an actor would be heard from just one speaker.

Many mixers will also allow several mixes to be made by a single mixer and then sent to different places. When taping a performance, I have found it very useful to have one mix going to the house speakers and a second mix going to a video tape recorder. This allows both mixes to be adjusted without interfering with the other. A second use of this feature is to provide actors with a stage monitor so that they can hear themselves and any musical accompaniment when they are singing. It is often hard for actors to hear a sound system that has been optimized for the audience.

VOLTAGE CONTROLLED AMPLIFIERS

There was a great little mixer built by JBL that had a wonderful feature built into it. How do you handle a situation where a sound is too loud or an actor must change costumes without the microphone amplifying the rustling of fabric? If a sound technician is available, just turn down the sound; simple, huh? But what if one isn't? The answer is a Voltage Controlled Amplifier (VCA for short). These are basically remote control volume controls. They can be controlled by a computer exactly as a light dimmer is controlled. Tape deck too loud? A VCA connected to a computer can turn it down. Want to mute a microphone for that costume change? With a VCA this is simple. Sadly, this particular mixer is no longer made, but several companies make add-on VCAs. As the following example will show, they are well worth their cost.

When we first began producing plays here, we would spend hours in a studio with the director getting the various sound levels just right on a master tape. We would then make the show tape and head for the stage to try it out. Invariably the director would tell us that part of the tape was too loud and the rest was too soft, so back we went into the studio. This would happen several more times until the director finally, grudgingly, would say a tape was acceptable, but not great. No more of that! All we do now is tape all the sounds needed for a play at a constant level and then program the computer to raise or lower the volumes with VCAs until the director is satisfied.

Another advantage of VCAs involves timing. What if a scene were to need background music or sound effects? It might be possible to time the scene exactly and then record sound to match. The only problem with this is that different actors may take slightly more or less time to play the scene or something may happen to slow down the scene. Rather than having the sound run out too soon or carry over into the next scene, just record more sound than necessary and use VCAs controlled by a computer to fade out the sound at the appropriate moment. There will most likely be a light change at the same time and remember that VCAs act just like dimmers for sound.

AMPLIFIERS AND SPEAKERS

There are so many amplifiers and speakers available that I really don't have any recommendations. Any good quality amplifier and speaker should work just fine. Do remember that balanced equipment is less likely to be affected by interference or to cause hums. Small speakers are less obtrusive but often have less bass than larger speakers. A nice compromise is to use a speaker system consisting of two small speakers to provide the stereo sound and a third speaker called a sub-woofer to provide the bass. The sub-woofer can be placed practically anywhere near the stage and so is easy to hide.

A NOTE ON MIDI

I will just mention that there is a very elaborate system of sound control called MIDI. A MIDI system uses something called a sequencer that can start and stop sound devices, mix signals, and fade volumes. I have never used MIDI although it is very popular, especially with musicians. The system I will be recommending here, called Trax, incorporates all the controls of MIDI and extends them to include lighting, slides, video, and more. Before purchasing any equipment, you may want to find out about MIDI and see if it might be better for you.

PUTTING IT ALL TOGETHER

So, how do you go about putting all this equipment together? Fortunately, things can be purchased as funds become available; it is not necessary to get everything at once. The needs of a particular program many require some things but not others or some items may have been purchased already. Here is a possible plan to augment a theater program with technology.

Probably the best place to start is with lighting. Purchase enough theatrical fixtures to light the stage and then, when possible, add dimmers. You will need a light board to control the dimmers. At first, the lights can be left at a setting or controlled by someone off stage. Next you may wish to add sound. To do this, you will need a tape deck, amplifier, and speakers. The deck can be controlled by the built-in remote control or a radio frequency slide projector remote control can be modified to start the deck. Remember that certain tape decks will stop themselves at the proper place on the tape. You may want to consider adding microphones. If so, you will need one transmitter and one receiver for each actor and a sound mixer to combine the signals from the tape deck and the microphones. When you add microphones you will probably need a 1/3 octave equalizer or a feedback eliminator to allow the microphones to be most effective.

If you have someone on staff who is good with computers, you may want to create your own program to control the lights and tape deck. The remote control that you had connected to the tape deck can be reused to cue the computer which in turn will now control the tape deck. If you add VCAs to your sound system you will be able to adjust the sound volumes through the computer.

As your system becomes more elaborate and your productions begin to use more technology, you can consider adding other pieces of equipment such as video tape decks, slide projectors, strobe lights, and so forth. Really, at this point, the only limitation is your imagination. You may decide that a talking mixmaster would be perfect for your play on modern inventions. Hide a speaker next to the mixmaster, connect the mixmaster's motor to a computer controlled switch, focus a special light on the mixmaster and control the whole thing with the hidden remote control linked to your computer. Now your actor can talk as long as he or she wishes and exactly on cue, the mixmaster will light up, turn on, and answer the actor.

But what if you cannot modify your own computer?

Re-enter *Leonardo*

By the time of *Leonardo* the Museum of Science in Boston had used its computerized system for over ten years. It was developed for a play about The Mary Rose, the flag ship of Henry VIII which was being preserved by underwater archaeologists. We wanted lights to signify changes in scene but could not afford a lighting technician and a professional actor. Our solution was to modify an Apple computer (remember them?) with a jury-rigged program and (then) commercially available digital-to-analog cards.

Why is it that everything is always harder than you think it will be? We did not get the system up and running in time for the first show so I had to lie prone under the 18-inch-high stage operating the light board and strain to hear the actor's cues over the (very loud) sound of his foot steps. By the next performance, things were working satisfactorily. That inauspicious start initiated our use of computers.

It has proven to be a good system generally, but there have been some problems. Some actors find it difficult to use the system; one actor in fact, refused to use it. We had another unfortunate instance when I had mistakenly set up two nearby systems to use the same transmitter frequencies. Actors in one play were causing light changes in the other. Needless to say, the actors had quite a bit to say to me after that. Occasionally the transmitter does not work properly and either a cue is missed or skipped. In either case, the results can be disastrous. If a play changes mood frequently, as ours often do, imagine the effect when an actor has a quiet, serious scene only to find that the computer has started bright, perky music in the background! Yet, all-in-all, the system has worked perfectly in thousands of performances. It is simply necessary to realize that with advanced technology come advanced ways for things to go wrong. I saw Miss Saigon, one of the most computer-controlled plays of all time, when the helicopter got stuck as it was supposedly flying away from the American compound. It stayed there in mid air until the end of the act.

For *Leonardo* our system controlled 18 dimmers connected to about 30 lighting fixtures, two tape decks, six VCAs, and several motors. It could do nothing more. We got into this situation because of the demands of the play. The playwright and director, Jon Lipsky, envisioned the play as mirroring Leonardo's mind: constantly shifting from one idea to another; full of schemes to test those ideas; and always, always, observing the world around him. It consisted of a series of short vignettes in which an actor, guided by a mysterious mask-maker, learned to think and see as Leonardo himself did. It was a very ambitious play and, I believe, a valuable way for visitors to end their stay at the exhibit. The problem was each vignette had its own lighting and sound effect. It was the sound that almost did us in.

As I said above, we could have timed each vignette and recorded the appropriate amount of music. However, we had four casts of two actors doing the play each hour for six months (as I said, *Leonardo* seemed larger than life) and Jon and I knew the actors would take different amounts of time to do the scenes. We decided instead to use two tape decks for alternating sound effects. The first deck would play the first bit of sound. When the actors reached the end of that scene, one of the actors would hit the remote control which changed the lights and lowered the sound on the first tape deck with a VCA. The second tape deck would start and play the second sound. This went on for about 20 sound cues.

Why not just stop the first deck, advance it to the next selection, and then start it again? That would be ideal if tape decks had a system similar to CDs that would allow them to cue up to exactly the correct place on a tape, but, unfortunately, except for DAT players, they don't. Instead we had to have two separate decks, a VCA for the two channels of each deck, a switch to start each deck, and another to rewind the decks so that the show would automatically reset at the end. These controls started to add up and by that time in front of the darkened stage just before the opening, we did not have any more capacity in our system.

If I had it to do over, I would not have done it this way. The whole program was just too complicated. The actors, bless them, tried their best to work with the many cues, but at times, they would try to go on to a scene before the tape deck (last used two scenes ago) had finished its previous piece. When this happened, disaster would strike. The program, which had no way of telling that the sound was now out of sync, would continue to do what it had been programmed to do, start a piece of music, regardless of the consequences. The actors were marvelous at making the best of the situation, which, incidentally, is another reason why I prefer live presenters to canned performances. As much as I was comfortable with the system and grateful to it for a decade's worth of plays, I knew this was going to be the last time we used that system. It was time for Trax.

TRAX: DEUS EX MACHINA

As it happened, *Leonardo* not only caused the problem but also provided the solution. I had been hearing about a system named Trax developed by a company called Dataton. The producer of a multimedia "object theater" that we used to introduce the visitors to the Leonardo exhibit used Trax to run her show. I was given the equipment when the exhibit closed.

Trax is an off-the-shelf software program that runs on a Macintosh computer and can control, it seems, almost anything through dedicated hardware. You don't need anyone familiar with computers to use it. Just load it into a Mac, follow the directions to connect tape decks, dimmers, slide projectors, and so forth, and you are set to start. It works by running time lines (its "trax") which initiate cues. As I learned about the program, several advantages became apparent. One of the great advantages of Trax is that many devices provide feedback to the computer so that the system knows what is really going on out there, not just what is supposed to be going on. I liked it already. Another advantage is that you can set up logical conditions for different cues. If you want one thing to happen only if another thing has happened, you are all set. A third big advantage, perhaps the biggest of all, is that the program no longer must be linear. It is easy to jump all over the place. Here are some of the ways I am currently using the program and some ways I hope to use it in the future.

Let's start with that sound problem we had in *Leonardo*. The problem occurred because there is no reliable way to cue up a tape deck in fast-forward mode. (Digital Audio Tape decks do have a way.) These days it is possible to record CDs and use them as we used to use tapes. With this system, any point on a CD can be located to a fraction of a second and the player can then be started. It is also possible to give the CD player a time to stop. If you have several sequential sound cues with time in between each sound, just tell the player when to start and when to stop. It will just sit there waiting for the next cue. Better yet, the player can be started at a point and, at any later time, the system can fade out the sound, jump instantly to another point on the CD, either earlier or later, and start playing again. This feature alone would have solved our problems in *Leonardo*.

We sometimes have a problem with actors hitting a cue too soon. With the old system, there was nothing we could do about it; the cue happened, like it or not. With this system, we are making use of another button on the transmitter. The first button is considered the "go" button. When it is pressed, the computer begins a time line which causes one or 100 cues to occur. The second button is considered the "hold" button. When it is pressed, the current time line stops and any cues, such as a light fade or a sound cue, stop as well. In the future, I would like to change this button into a "back" button. This will allow the actor to return to the beginning of the incorrectly hit cue, effectively canceling the mistake. This is only going to be possible because of the use of CDs and their ability to be cued at any point, earlier or later, than the current position. Dimmers, sound, motors, slides, everything will return to their correct position. Neat, huh?

A "skip" button can also be made very easily. This button can either skip to the next cue or to any cue in the entire program. One of our plays begins with a slide show. Sometimes it is necessary to cut the show short, so the actor simply presses the skip button and the program goes to the end of the show and continues from there. It is done smoothly, without any glitches, and the audience has no idea that it happened. Another program is set up to be shortened at a particular point. The presenter, not an actor, decides at that point if there is enough time to go through the entire program or if a particular demonstration should be skipped. This same method could be used for a play. The skip button does not even have to be a separate button. Since the system can be used to set up logical conditions, a single button can function in any number of ways by setting up "if-then" commands at different points in the play.

One of the most intriguing features of the system is the ability to have branching programs. At key points in a play, the actors (or the audience) can decide which way to go. For instances, a play can have many different endings depending on the audience's response to a question. As long as the actors remember where they are in a program and what comes next in all the different branches, there is no limit to the flexibility this method will provide. It is even possible to have colored lights go on at the back of the house to remind actors where they are.

Lights, sound, video disks, and slides will all follow along with this system as it branches because they are all being told exactly where they should be, not simply that they should do the next thing. This non-linearity is tremendously exciting to me, although I am a bit concerned what our director will do now that I no longer have to keep him connected with reality. I'm convinced that given time and a little ingenuity, anything can be done.

The coordinator of our theater program and I have worked together for years. We have come to know each other well and what we can expect from each other. I take care of the technology and she takes care of the performance values in each play. It has become a joke between us that not only does she dislike doing technical things, but if something technical is going to go wrong, it will probably happen to her.

Not too long ago I had finished programming a show with our new system and then started another project. The coordinator mentioned to me that she would really like to have some changes made to one scene, but I told her it would have to wait a bit until I had some more time. A couple of days later I had the time and asked her what she wanted done.

She told me not to bother, she had made the changes herself.

RESPONSE TO *Museum Theater and Technology*

DALE JONES, INSTITUTE FOR LEARNING INNOVATION

I was quite transfixed and inspired by Mike Alexander's writing on museum theater and technology. While I have not had the pleasure of seeing any of his productions, I have enviously talked to him and other staff at the Museum of Science about their equipment and technical expertise. At one point I even tried to manipulate a temporary exhibit I was curating so it would require computers, sound, lighting, and Mike's technical expertise. My plan was to remove the equipment from the exhibit after it closed and incorporate it into the museum theater program at the former Baltimore City Life Museums, which up to that point had existed without technology.

I'm not opposed to the technical aspects of theater, but our museum theater program started in a museum where technology was completely out of place. The 1840 House was essentially a reproduction of a home in which there were small rooms and no modern intrusions like lights and electricity. To include lights, sound, and all the accompanying technology was impossible and unnecessary. Being seen or heard was not an issue. Our actors were never more than eight feet away and often within arms-length of the audience (in one performance a visitor standing behind me actually rested her hand on my shoulder as I sat on a sofa). Our scripts and performances were naturalistic, and we had to communicate without any technical assistance.

Such remembrances bring me to the point of my reactions to Mike's comments. While the technical aspects he imbeds in a production are wonderful, (and I would add necessary in museums like his), they are neither needed nor appropriate for effective museum theater in small historic sites and most smaller institutions.

What is necessary for success are the elements that are common to both the Museum of Science and to smaller venues in which I have worked—a solid script, excellent directors and actors, and a staff advocate with an appreciation of the power and magic of theater. More about that below.

Clear disadvantages of using a system as described by Mike are the expense and complication. The technical hardware needed for a such a program is not extraordinarily expensive, but lights, gels, dimmers, microphones, amplifiers, speakers, computers, and other equipment can be costly. A more significant obstacle for most smaller institutions would be to find someone with the technical expertise to program and maintain everything.

Lighting and sound are also inappropriate for the small, intimate spaces often found in museums. In many of the historical dramatizations I have done, part of our goal was to immerse the visitor in the time period being interpreted. The obvious benefits of lighting, sound, and the accompanying equipment to productions such as Leonardo would detract from the suspension of disbelief we are trying to achieve (although in Mike's situation they clearly assist that suspension of disbelief). If I were just starting out to produce museum theater, I might feel overwhelmed at the thought of not only finding funds for a playwright, director, and actors, but also needing to find funding and expertise to add the technical aspects suggested by Mike.

The reality of producing good museum theater, however, is that in most cases, all you need are a good director and solid actors, a well-written script, costumes and props, and a determination to succeed. These elements are, of course, the same base-line requirements for any successful theatrical presentation, whether on Broadway, at a large science museum, or at a small historic site with a staff of one.

CHAPTER 10

WORKING WITH COMMUNITIES:
BUILDING BRIDGES THROUGH REMINISCENCE THEATRE

Sherry Anne Chapman, Glenbow Museum

Bridge building. What does it require? Two places or bodies that wish to communicate with one another. Some imagination for designing the connecting system. And then, the actual threads of connection, the planking so to speak, so that residents of each place can cross the bridge to meet.

As a museum professional who has focused on the use of museum theatre as a learning medium and who has increasingly come to work with older adults, hearing of the existence of reminiscence theatre was a moment of wonder. I felt as though a single road, where once there had been two paths, had materialized before me offering new direction. Reminiscence programming with older adults and intergenerational groups has opened up for me a new way of looking at museum work. For the purposes of this chapter, I will focus on reminiscence theatre as a bridge-building medium between museums and their communities. Reference will be made to the Glenbow Museum where I work and the community of Calgary, Alberta, Canada and to Age Exchange Theatre Trust and its Reminiscence Centre in London, England. In visiting Age Exchange in the spring of 1998, I had an opportunity to observe how its staff and volunteers work with their community and I learned some of the benefits of doing so. The chapter will relate some of the ideas that I have, following Age Exchange's example of bridge building.

Glenbow is western Canada's largest museum. Holding significant collections of Native Canadian history, contemporary and historical art, military history, western Canadian history, and mineralogy, Glenbow also houses an extensive research library and one of Canada's largest nongovernmental archives. With more than 120 full- and part-time staff, Glenbow offers visitors a unique mix of exhibitions and programs. More than 200,000 people visit Glenbow each year, with millions more viewing Glenbow's travelling exhibitions throughout western Canada and around the world. Glenbow is an innovative, open, and self-reliant organization where visitors find meaning and value, and where learners of all ages delight in exploring the diversity of the human experience.

Through the last two years, Glenbow has reviewed its programming for older adults and has initiated new ideas including reminiscence programming, a relatively new area of museum work in North America. In 1996, a recreation therapist suggested to Glenbow that the museum had the objects and images that were needed for therapeutic reminiscence in the community. At about the same time, the museum learned about a reminiscence kit program at Glasgow Museums' Open Museum.

In October 1997, the Glenbow Reminiscence Kit Team comprised of museum staff and community health-care professionals launched Glenbow's Reminiscence Kit program. The goal of this outreach program is:

To loan mini-museums in suitcases to continuing care facilities and others to promote discussion and to stimulate past experiences with older, isolated individuals. The items included in each kit date from the 1920s through the 1950s and are chosen to trigger memories from specific time periods or situations in an older person's life.

Twelve themed kits were created with duplicate and triplicate objects from the collection, archival images, audio tapes of popular songs, and familiar scents. Suggestions for using the kits were included for borrowers' reference. (See Appendix C.)

The kits have been extremely well received and are loaned out across the province. Now, in 1998, as the coordinator of the kit team, I am realizing that the kits are just the beginning of a strong and mutually beneficial relationship between Glenbow and the community, all based upon the bridge planking that is reminiscence.

How did reminiscence objects and images become such a community need? In 1963, the American psychiatrist, Robert Butler, published a paper describing the life review process of older adults.[1] He observed that reminiscence played a role in that process of sorting through the experiences of one's life. While reminiscence may happen privately or casually between two people, reminiscence in group sessions is also therapeutic. 'Looking back' has been recognized as a constructive part of later life.

Reminiscence is a recounting of life stories. It can be a doorway for communication for a person with dementia or a medium for the collection of community history. It can be used for personal enjoyment and education. James Magee writes that reminiscence occurs when an individual, often with a listener, recalls an experience from his or her past and recovers the emotions associated with the event.[2]

Memories shared around a common theme may spark conversation in individuals who have been isolated from living on their own or from an inability to express themselves. Shared reminiscence demonstrates that the listeners value the memories and, thus, value the owner of those memories such that: 'Your memories are important; they matter; you matter. I wish to listen to you.' Reminiscence may renew an individual's self-confidence and independence. Therapeutic reminiscence can help to improve the quality of life of an older adult.

Therapeutic reminiscence is used to support people with dementia. Alzheimer Disease is the leading cause of dementia for Canadians 65 years of age and older.[3] While short-term memory is lost first in the disease process,[4] the use of an older object, a familiar scent, or a song can awaken long-term memories and help a listener to understand the individual's 'present.' With the progressive memory loss, one's sense of identity is gradually destroyed. For the person with dementia, reminiscence can be a way to communicate through that which is still familiar—objects, images, sounds that date back to earlier times in peoples' lives. Glenbow's reminiscence kit program was designed particularly with people with dementia in mind.

"Winter Warmers" reminiscence theatre piece in the multi-layered Winter Warmers project supported by the Department of Health, help the Aged and the London Boroughs Grant Scheme. The project comprise extensive interviews across four London Boroughs, a three-dimensional exhibition in the Reminiscence Theatre, a professional touring theatre show and a book of photos and memories. *Photograph by Alex Schweitzer. Photo courtesy of Age Exchange Theatre Trust. London.*

In the late 1970s and early 1980s, Mick Kemp, a British architect concerned with older adults' residential homes, led the Reminiscence Aids Project which resulted in 'Recall,' a set of slides and sounds of East-End London intended for use as reminiscence triggers.[5] Later, additional sets of slides were created to reflect life experiences elsewhere in Britain. In time, reminiscence workers found that photographs and objects worked equally well if not better for sparking reminiscence than showing slides in a darkened room. In the 1980s, therapists throughout Britain began to ask museums for artifacts that might be used for reminiscence work.

In 1977, a psychiatrist and a university drama lecturer in Devon, England, believed that theatre that brought to life older adults' memories would also act as a trigger for further reminiscence. Following a pilot, a full-time company called Fair Old Times was created. Through 1981, it produced 12 productions developed from local reminiscences. Each performance was designed to spark new reminiscences.[6]

In the early 1980s, Pam Schweitzer was an education officer in an older people's London home. She was working with older adults and children using drama. By 1983, she had launched Age Exchange Theatre Trust as a professional reminiscence theatre touring company. Since then, as the founder and artistic director of Age Exchange, Schweitzer has led the company through 30 different productions and several theatre-in-education programs based on reminiscence. The Age Exchange Youth Theatre was established in 1985 and a company of older adults, The Good Companions, was established in 1993.

Through the years, Age Exchange has evolved into an arts organization that 'aims to improve the quality of life of older people by emphasising the value of their reminiscences to old and young.'[7] The Reminiscence Centre was opened in London in 1987 for people to drop-in and visit the hands-on museum and rotating exhibitions. Age Exchange publishes reminiscence resource books and collections of reminiscences from the theatre projects and offers intergenerational programming and reminiscence training.

Schweitzer defines reminiscence theatre as theatre that is derived from the memories of older people. For a production, Age Exchange works with the reminiscences of many individuals surrounding a theme. Those memories are incorporated verbatim into a script which when performed is intended to stimulate and entertain older and mixed-age audiences and to evoke further reminiscence.[8] Age Exchange attempts to reflect the memories of the rich cultural diversity of London's elders.

Age Exchange is the coordinating member of the European Reminiscence Network established in 1995. Among its important projects is the promotion of reminiscence theatre. The 1995 Network Reminiscence Theatre Festival, A Time to Remember, was hosted by Age Exchange. One hundred and fifty participants from 20 cities shared their reminiscence theatre work surrounding the theme of the Second World War.[9] Most of the participants were older adults and many of them attended as performers with reminiscence theatre groups from England (Age Exchange), Greece, Denmark, Germany, France, Italy, Taiwan, and the United States. The latter group, Footsteps of the Elders, from Ohio, was established in 1994.

Here are just a few of the many Age Exchange productions drawn from *Age Exchange Annual Reports* 1988-89 to 1996-97. The shows have been performed in Britain

End of the war celebrations in "Cheers" by the Age Exchange group (The Good Companions and Age Exchange Youth Theatre) at the European Reminiscence Network Reminiscence Theatre Festival "A Time to Remember," Age Exchange, London: also performed in Germany. *Photograph by Alex Schweitzer. Photo courtesy of Age Exchange Theatre Trust. London.*

but have also toured Europe since 1993. Performances are given to seniors clubs, community centres, seniors' residences, continuing-care facilities, theatres, and other organizations.

1983 *Fifty Years Ago Show*—Age Exchange's first production.

1984 *A Place to Stay*—This show was based upon reminiscences (in eight languages) of the experiences of elders from across London's culturally diverse population.

1988 *Good Morning Children*—Age Exchange's first theatre-in-education program was set in a recreated 1920s school room exhibit at the Reminiscence Centre. The role play show took place in the morning and then, in the afternoon, the students met with some of the older adults whose reminiscences were included in the show.

1989 *Across the Irish Sea*—This production reflected the reminiscences of Irish pensioners living in London. The publication sold particularly well.

1994 *Grandmother's Footsteps*—This was a joint production between The Good Companions and Age Exchange Youth Theatre.

1998 *Can We Afford the Doctor?*—This 1985 show was revived in 1988 and again in 1998 to celebrate the 40th and 50th anniversaries of the National Health Service, respectively.

1998 *Routes*—This 1993 show based on the experiences of Punjabi elders was revived for the March 1998 European Reminiscence Network Festival and Conference on Reminiscence and Ethnic Elders, *Journey of a Lifetime*, focusing on the reminiscences of ethnic minority elders from across Europe and the United States. Age Exchange hosted the conference.

Having provided some context for reminiscence theatre, I will now turn to the case study portion of the chapter. I have chosen to focus on one of Age Exchange's reminiscence theatre productions, *What Did You Do in the War, Mum?* and on a Glenbow museum theatre program, *Victory Matinee*, to compare and contrast bridge building.

In 1985, Age Exchange debuted its show, *What Did You Do in the War, Mum?* by Joyce Holliday. It considers women's work in the Second World War and includes verbatim reminiscence, documentary material, and popular songs of the war.[10]

I had the opportunity to watch a videotape recording of the production. Before the play begins, one of the women whose memories were included in the play is interviewed. She was a member of the Women's Auxiliary Air Force during the war and she responded to Age Exchange's call for wartime experiences. Pam Schweitzer visited and interviewed her. As well as her reminiscences, one of her poems from the war was used as the lyrics for an original song in the play. Through the collecting of her reminiscences, Pam and the woman built a bridge. The latter helped to inform the production and then later, she witnessed the animation of her own memories. She said that she was interested in remaining involved with Age Exchange. Many women's memories were incorporated into the script. Many bridges were built in this manner.

Following the interview, the video recording then presented the play, which ran for about 1 hour and 20 minutes. The five actresses moved through many characters and costume and set changes. They sang popular songs from the war and often shifted from a reminiscence perspective of storytelling to live action dialogue. The play ended with the beautifully presented song that begins with the line, 'When the lights go on again all over the world. . . .' After the applause, the actresses immediately started singing another period song and began encouraging the audience to join in. The video recording ended there.

When *What Did You Do in the War, Mum?* was revived in 1992/93, 70 performances were given in England, Scotland, Belgium, Germany, Denmark, and France. In the *Age Exchange Annual Report* 1992/93, Pam Schweitzer wrote:

Again, we have been extremely warmly received so far, with audiences identifying strongly with the material, even where they might have been our wartime opponents. The audiences were keen to discuss the content of the play as well as our approach to play-making through reminiscences, and again we felt that we had worried unnecessarily about possible difficulties we might encounter in discussing the war years, especially with older people in Germany.[11]

At Glenbow, the Reminiscence Kit Team members have discussed the subject of the wars of this century and the need to support older adults in their reminiscences of those times. In the Age Exchange training courses in which I participated, I learned that reminiscence sessions should be set up to support participants through the memories that they choose to share. People should never be forced to speak of that which they do not wish. They will share the memories and emotions with which they feel comfortable as evident in Pam's above observation.

In the *Age Exchange Annual Report* for 1993-1994, *What Did You Do in the War, Mum?* is reported as playing another 88 performances again throughout Britain and Europe!

Describing Age Exchange's productions generally, Pam Schweitzer has written that the actors usually range in age from 25 to 40 years and represent the older adults whose reminiscences are included in the play as their younger selves. The majority of members of the audiences of older adults often have varying degrees of dementia. Their responses reflect yet another stage of bridge building:

They invariably take the opportunity to share their own memories with the actors, the care-givers, and each other after the show, revealing to staff and to each other biographical information and insight which is new for those who have been caring for them. Very often the staff in the places where we play are surprised by the degree and quality of response.[12]

Enjoying Glenbow Reminiscence Kit #9: "Music, Games, and Fun." (From left to right) Eunice Congo, Verna Johnson, Don Johnson, George Congo. *Photograph by Anita Dammer. Photo courtesy of Glenbow Museum*

Through reminiscence theatre, new bridges of communication are built between the older adults and Age Exchange, between residents and their care givers, and between the care-givers and Age Exchange. Pam notes that often, following a performance, care-givers ask for more information on therapeutic reminiscence; Age Exchange is able to support them through reminiscence training and programming options.

In an article in *Reminiscence*, the magazine of the European Reminiscence Network, Angelika Trilling, a planner of social services for older people and of training for care-givers, wrote about the performance when it visited Kassel, Germany. She observed:

The show succeeded in provoking apparently fairly similar memories among the older Germans as it had among the older British audiences. More fascinating still: it taught younger Germans in the audience a new way of looking at their elders' war reminiscences.[13]

Through the call for and collection of memories from the community to the animated discussions following each performance, everyone involved in the reminiscence theatre experience gains new insight into themselves and others as personal living history is shared.

Turning to Glenbow, in 1995, we produced *Victory Matinee*, a specially commissioned play reflecting the Canadian home front experience of the Second World War through the medium of a radio program typical of the time. The play was written by the local playwright, Rose Scollard, to comprise part of the programming for the special exhibition that Glenbow mounted to celebrate the 50th anniversary of the end of the Second World War. *Memories of War, Dreams of Peace* presented the experiences of Canadians both at home and abroad during the war and included, as label text and sound bites, brief transcribed reminiscences of members of the war generation. Some of the older adults who were interviewed about the war were recruited as 'first-person' interpreters for the exhibit during its run. They participated in school programs and spent time stationed in the exhibit talking casually with visitors about their own and the visitors' experiences.

Victory Matinee was a 1940s style live radio show styled after a Canadian radio program of the period, *The Happy Gang*. The play was written for casual weekend visitors of all ages and ran on a monthly basis through the five-month run of the exhibit. Popular period music was included in the script.

Four actors, two women and two men, represented radio personalities and guests and related to the audience as a live studio audience. Visitors were prompted to respond with large cue cards as a live radio audience would have been prompted during the period. On the opening night of the exhibition and the play, CBC Radio Canada, also celebrating an anniversary, presented a live-to-air broadcast from Glenbow's galleries interviewing museum staff and older adults involved in the project and transmitting the play live.

After each monthly performance, the actors used the play as a springboard for discussion to create an opportunity for visitors to share with the actors and other visitors their war memories as they or their family and friends remembered them. Visitors approached the actors to say, for example, that they remembered wartime radio shows or that, as with one visitor, she was an original member of Canada's overseas variety show, *The Army Show!* The program appealed not only to war generation visitors, but also to younger visitors who had a connection to the war through relatives and friends.

Summative data were collected through taped visitor interviews and questionnaires, attendance numbers, and staff feedback. Both visitors and Glenbow staff observed that the play communicated the ambience of the war years in western Canada. One visitor said that:

> The conversation afterwards and sharing by members of the audience were really interesting and wouldn't have occurred without the performance. Great for those of us who weren't around during the war years . . . helps us to relate to our elders. Good to have a 'war bride' as a resource person.

While *Victory Matinee* certainly sparked new reminiscences following the program, the playwright had written from her research of the period and from her personal memories of early childhood on the home front and her mother's memories. She did not have the depth and variety of reminiscences that could be made available through reminiscence sessions. Pam Schweitzer has commented that the reminiscences from which Age Exchange works are collected from many individuals. I can see that a collection of reminiscences will ensure that the most common elements tied to a specific theme are included in a script to spark the greatest number of new reminiscences possible.

From my perspective, *Victory Matinee* was not reminiscence theatre, as it was not developed directly from older peoples' reminiscence sessions. However, it was an engaging museum theatre program that sparked positive audience response.

Through the exhibition process and the presentation of *Victory Matinee*, bridges were built with individuals in the community. Could the number of bridges have been more extensive, though, and better built to ensure that the new relationships outlasted the project? Certainly, Glenbow does not have the resources that Age Exchange has developed through the years to support its reminiscence work

and the work of the community. Glenbow did not have a structure in place to support continued reminiscence relationships with the older adults who were interviewed for the project. However, at least one of those individuals did become a Glenbow volunteer and has remained associated with the organization since 1995. And, I am now aware of the greater concept of reminiscence programming and how to go about supporting such relationships through time.

While Glenbow viewed *Victory Matinee* as a successful program for engaging visitors, I believe that had I known of the premise of reminiscence theatre in 1995, I would have chosen this approach. The reminiscence collection process might have built bridges with many more people of the war generation in Calgary, such that a 'buy-in' and supportive network might have been created. More families and friends might have heard about the project and been interested in the theatre product. Continuing care facilities and seniors' residences might have been interested enough to book the program.

While I write with hindsight, I am much inspired. Glenbow was on a good track in 1995. I recall the program's strong points and think forward to future opportunities. To celebrate 1999 as the International Year of Older Persons with the theme 'Towards a Society for All Ages,' Glenbow is hoping to expand its current programming for older adults. I can imagine launching reminiscence museum theatre at Glenbow following Age Exchange's example. Reminiscence sessions would be established surrounding a particular theme to collect older adults' memories, and then a scenario or script would be developed to incorporate them verbatim.

Why build bridges with older adults in the community through reminiscence theatre? In an aging population, the development of programming that recognizes the role of older adults as the sources of living memory and that supports them in their own lifelong learning makes sense. Museums are constantly striving to demonstrate their role in society. Rather than always assuming the role of the 'expert,' a museum can practise its role as facilitator of the collection and the celebration of reminiscences which are local social history. In the process, the museum will be informing its own collections and helping to pass that local history from one generation to the next. In the process, the museum will be helping to improve the quality of life of the older adults in its community through reminiscence.

Two places or bodies wish to communicate with each other. A bridge is envisioned. The supports are built and the planking is laid in place. The residents of each place can cross the bridge to meet. And then, the learning begins. Then, the ideas begin to flow.

ACKNOWLEDGEMENT:

I wish to thank Mrs. Joy Harvie Maclaren and the 1998 Glenbow Staff Scholarship Fund in her name for making my reminiscence research/study tour to Britain possible in the spring of 1998.

NOTES

1. Robert N. Butler, "The Life Review: an Interpretation of Reminiscence in the Aged," Psychiatry 26 (1963): 65-76.

2. James J. Magee, A Professional's Guide to Older Adults' Life Review: Releasing the Peace Within (Lexington, Massachusetts: Lexington Books, 1988), 2-3.

3. Dr. David Hogan, 'Alzheimer Disease and Research Update,' unpublished keynote address, the Alzheimer Society of Calgary 1998 Annual Conference, 'On Target: Changing Our Vision of Dementia Care,' Calgary, January 30, 1998.

4. Lisa Naess, 'Reminiscence Work with People with Dementia,' 'Reminiscence as a Means of Combatting Social Exclusion,' Introductory Papers for the Copenhagen Conference of the European Reminiscence Network, Nov. 15 - 17, 1996, DaneAge, Denmark and Age Exchange Theatre Trust, U.K., DGV European Commission, no page.

5. Joanna Bornat, 'Reminiscence Reviewed,' Reminiscence in Dementia Care, ed. Pam Schweitzer (London: Age Exchange, 1998), 45.

6. Baz Kershaw, 'Reminiscence Theatre: new techniques for old people,' Theatre Ireland, no issue or year, after 1981, no page number.

7. Pam Schweitzer, 'Age Exchange and Creative Reminiscence Projects, Especially with People with Dementia,' Reminiscence in Dementia Care, ed. Schweitzer, 138.

8. Pam Schweitzer, interview with author, Age Exchange Reminiscence Centre, The Bakehouse, London, April 29, 1998.

9. Age Exchange Annual Report 1995/96, 14.

10. 'Age Exchange's Programme of Activities for the European Year (of Older People and Solidarity between the Generations, 1993),' Reminiscence, January 1993, Issue 5, 7.

11. Age Exchange Annual Report 1992/93, 5.

12. Schweitzer, 'Age Exchange,' Reminiscence in Dementia Care, ed. Schweitzer, 139.

13. Angelika Trilling, 'Reminiscence: A German View,' Reminiscence, March 1994, Issue 7, 10.

RESPONSE TO *Working with Communities*

WENDY ELLEFSON, INTERPRETIVE PROGRAMS MANAGER,
MINNESOTA HISTORICAL SOCIETY

Museums are like castles. Built to endure and designed to inspire, they are citadels of knowledge, protectors of the past, and storehouses of treasure. They collect, preserve, and interpret human experience, selecting some stories for safekeeping within their walls and leaving others, for the moment, outside. But must museums, like castles, be surrounded by moats? As museums preserve and disseminate our human foibles and triumphs, too often the status of expert, the limits of a collection, and the history of doing things a certain way create a gulf between the castle and the community.

Most modern museums strive to be castles *without* moats. But as they seek inclusion, accessibility, and relevance within their communities, museums often discover an old and lingering chasm between potential and real audiences. One solution, as Sherry Anne Chapman suggests, is to build bridges between the museum and various communities through gallery theater programs. She illustrates the power of reminiscence theater to foster an exchange between museum and community, to push the museum away from its role as expert and toward the role of facilitator.

I would add that museum theater should be more than a bridge. Bridges collapse, need repair, and have limits to the weight they can hold. A successful program can drop a plank between one community group and the museum's education department, for example, only to have the bridge collapse when the community seeks validation elsewhere in the museum. How effective is a theater program that brings in family audiences if the museum lacks diaper-changing or nursing facilities? And what can the long-term impact of a piece produced with the local African-American community be if the museum does not actively collect stories and objects documenting the African-American experience, or if it acknowledges that community but once a year during Black History Month? Even the strongest bridge can collapse under the weight of such mixed messages.

Instead of just building bridges, museums need to fill the moat, and filling the moat requires museum-wide participation. Visitors, after all, see the castle as a whole, not as a collection of separate rooms or departments functioning independently of one another. The success of reminiscence theater wanes when an elderly visitor is frustrated by tiny, hard-to-read text produced by an exhibits department, and the triumph of culturally inclusive programming evaporates when museum security makes a point of trailing only the "Indian kids" or the "black kids." Communities will no longer tolerate museum access via certain bridges only. Getting rid of the gulf between museums and communities must be an institutional commitment, not a random effort of bridge building made by selected departments.

As part of a greater institutional commitment to serve varied audiences and communities, however, museum theater can make a big splash while doing its part to fill the moat. Theater actively communicates the emotions, ideas, and stories that can otherwise sit passively in an exhibit's objects, photographs, paintings, and text. It illuminates the people behind the objects and tells their stories through the medium of storytelling. It demands attention, and usually gets it. At the Minnesota History Center in Saint Paul, museum theater programs consistently receive notice in Twin Cities' media, often generating new interest in old exhibits. Within the exhibit galleries, many visitors may choose to walk past a panel of interpretive text but few, our research has demonstrated, will pass up a ten-minute live performance. Reaching out to communities with museum theater programs intensifies the drive to fill in the moat.

For a theater program to contribute successfully to a museum's moat-filling mission, it needs to be developed with patience, sincerity, skill, and commitment. Developers need to carefully consider the community representatives with whom they work. Do the representatives speak for the community? Are they well-known, respected members of the community, and are they, too, willing to be patient and demonstrate commitment even when the chasm seems bottomless? Hiring an Ojibwe playwright to create a script about Ojibwe traditions of wild ricing, I discovered the hard way, did not necessarily represent a positive step toward relationship-building with the American Indian community. We first should have gone to the elders on our Advisory Board and sought their advice. Their stories, after all, should be put forth by the representative of their choosing, not by the convenience of an easy-to-reach writer-for-hire.

Museum theater developers must also be able to listen and compromise. Chapman points out that during reminiscence sessions "people should never be forced to speak of that which they do not wish." This guideline applies equally well to any theater project that strives to deepen the trust between community and museum. The developer must accept the possibility of a final product very different from the originally conceived program. When we ask a community to share its stories, we must first listen to the stories they want to tell now, and then work toward the day when dialogue flows more freely, when community and museum are one and the same, sharing their tragedies and triumphs equally.

Castles (museums) no longer need moats to endure, inspire, and protect; yet old chasms continue to separate them from the many different audiences they strive to serve. We may, indeed, build bridges with museum theater programs. But if we fortify those theater programs with patience, the will to listen, and the commitment of the entire museum, we can fill the moat once and for all.

CHAPTER 11

EVALUATION OF THEATRE: EVALUATION IS A MUST!

Harry Needham
Canadian War Museum

WHY EVALUATE?

When resources are shrinking and retrenchment is in the air, there is no program area so readily identified as a candidate for the budgetary ax than the theatre program. Evaluation is not only a good thing to do—it is an essential weapon for self-defence!

Let's face it—theatre is, for most institutions, an innovative approach to interpretation. It can be comparatively expensive, especially if scripts, sets, and costumes, or the theatrical program itself are commissioned from outside contractors. There are all too many museum professionals who wonder, even today, if *any* kind of live interpretation is necessary, let alone live *theatre*!

I would argue, though, that we ought to be evaluating for more fundamental reasons.

In the past 50 years, we have worked hard to establish the connection between visitors and the wisdom that resides in our institutions, be they museums, zoos, aquariums, or art galleries. We have developed labels that visitors can actually read without benefit of a classical education and which, in a few cases, they can even relate to their own experience or, in rarer cases, from which they might derive humour! We have used pictures and sound and motion pictures to help communicate things that mere words cannot. We've tried interactive components in some of our exhibitions and when we have done so, it has often been with a "Gee Whiz! Why didn't we think of this before?" realization of their potential impact. We have experimented with a wide variety of forms of live interpretation, costumed and not, and a few of us have even experimented with the notion that theatre can be used to turn information that might otherwise be "dead" or, at least, deadly dull, into something which lives and breathes and has an impact on our visitors.

But is any of this really new—or are we simply getting back to "first principles"? Is educational theatre—perhaps

the most inherently powerful arrow in our quiver—all that far removed in its connective purpose from the medieval morality play? For that matter, can we expect that the advent of CD-ROMs or virtual museums to which the visitors can connect via the Internet will really represent anything other than new technologies employed for a very traditional purpose?

Do we really know how much of what we already do works? Or where it works? Or how? Or for which audience segments? We see other institutions try these ideas and we institute our own versions of them, confident that, if it is good for others, it is good for us too. But do we ever try to measure their effects? Not very often.

I'd like to believe that most of us take our jobs pretty seriously. We have dedicated ourselves to helping connect the visitors to the wisdom, or we wouldn't be working in the madhouses we do! I am therefore convinced that our primary motivation is concern that we're doing the very best we can to ensure our theatre programs help visitors connect to the wisdom that lies in wait for them.

Member of Canadian Museum of Civilization theatre company interpreting Haida Indian legend Haida House of Museum. *Photo by: Harry Foster/Steve Darby of Canadian Museum of Civilization.*

As I have suggested above, those who look over our shoulders are now demanding that we be accountable—in new and uncomfortable ways. They are asking, for the first time, for proof that we are doing the great job we have said we are—and we are discovering that, not only do we not have the proof they want, but that we aren't too clear how to obtain that proof.

Let me say here and now that I have very little time for most of the performance measures that museums, particularly some American museums, have tried to put in place—measures which focus overwhelmingly on matters of efficiency and/or economy. Our focus ought more properly to be on measures of effectiveness. I believe in accountability (what manager can object to it?), but as a manager, I am far more concerned with how well a theatre program connects the visitors with the wisdom than on counting the number of artifacts per square metre of exhibition space or the ratio of size of kitchen staff to numbers of sandwiches sold in the coffee shop.

What can visitor studies do to help us improve the connection between the visitors and the wisdom? What, in particular, can such studies do to optimize the effectiveness of our educational theatre programs? How can evaluation be used to prove (or disprove) the effectiveness of such programs—and their indispensability?

KNOW YOUR VISITOR

For a start, visitor studies can tell us who our visitors really are. Are they local residents or are they tourists? If they're local people, what are their characteristics? What do they want—or need?

If the visitors to whom we must connect are tourists, where do they come from and how well can they use the institutional language or languages to connect to the wisdom communicated by our educational theatre program? How old are they? How well-educated? Are they male or female? Do they come alone or in groups? Have they been here before? How many times over how many years? Are there special characteristics about which you need to know? For example, if you are a military museum, you will probably want to know how many of your visitors are veterans—and their families. How are all these things changing and why?

I cannot believe that you can offer any effective interpretation program (and this indeed includes educational theatre) unless you know the basic facts about your clientele. Yet, I know of many institutions that do not even possess this essential knowledge, and remember, please, that we have not yet asked them a single question about our actual program.

Many visitor studies in heritage institutions then go on to ask questions about visitor needs and interests, use of programs and satisfaction with the program or one or another aspect of it. This is certainly useful information—for *any* program. I suggest, though, that in a relatively innovative and oft-challenged program such as educational theatre, evaluation has to go a *lot* deeper—to be the kind of study known in the trade as a program evaluation. Only this form of evaluation will give you the information you need to improve the program and that can be used to demonstrate its effectiveness and to protect it from those who do not understand it. If you can't demonstrate to the high-priced help that you have truly challenged the need for such a program, you will be a potential candidate for the budgetary axe. To challenge your program, you need to look at four things:

1) MANDATE

Evaluation can examine the mandate or mission of your theatre program or programs, weigh these against the mandate or mission of your institution in general and answer a very fundamental question—Does this program make sense for this institution? For an established program, you should ask a slightly different question—If it once made sense, does it still do so? You may find that it doesn't.

An examination of the program's mandate should be the starting point of any evaluation of an interpretation—or, for that matter—any other kind of program.

I think that when you look at a program's mandate and the other three issues I'm going to mention, it is essential to do so in relation to all other programs of the institution. Interpretation is there as a connection and that connection is highly dependent upon its interface with other programs and with the wisdom of the institution itself, as much as with the visitors. If this interface—or a related connection—is not working properly, it may subvert the success of your interpretation connection. In this case, improving your own program will be a waste of time and money. It makes little sense to set the broken leg, when blood is dripping down the arm! For example, there is no point in improving your theatre program if problems in museum signage and advertising mean that the visitors don't know about it or can't find it.

First-person interpretation of the Canadian square timber trade of the 19th century by member of CMC theatre company in the timber shanty of the Museum's Canada Hall. *Photo by: Harry Foster/Steve Darby of Canadian Museum of Civilization.*

2) OBJECTIVES ACHIEVEMENT

The second thing you need to look at is how well your program's objectives are being achieved, again viewed against the objectives of the institution, writ large. The question to be asked is this—Is the theatre program doing what we thought it would do?

After doing evaluation for more than 15 years, my conclusion is that the most significant problems in a program are usually centred around objectives. They may not even exist to any recognizable degree—the program is like the child Topsy in Harriet Beecher Stowe's novel of slavery *Uncle Tom's Cabin*, who said she never had had a mammy or a pappy—she "jest growed." Objectives may not exist at all; or they may merely be inadequate, inaccurate, unclear, and/or misunderstood. In *any* of these circumstances, the program is unlikely to do what was intended.

Some years ago, we evaluated the programs of the Canadian War Museum. When we looked at its mandate, we discovered that its management and staff saw themselves as constituting a memorial to Canada's war dead

and to the nation's military history—a worthy mission, to be sure, but should a war museum not serve to educate and, in doing so, to influence the behaviour of future generations? It then came as no surprise, when we came to examine the objectives of the museum's public programs, that the objectives that dealt with interpreting and educating ranked well down the list of priorities. Should we then have been surprised to find that it was only the veterans and the small group of military history buffs who frequented the museum and that most other potential visitors made no connection to it? Resetting the objectives and setting new program priorities have radically changed the museum's visitor base in four short years—and that is giving the museum a *growing*, instead of a shrinking, visitor population!

3) IMPACTS AND EFFECTS

There is a third question that can be asked: What is happening as a result of the program? In other words, what are its impacts and effects? *If* we have a clear and unambiguous mandate for the program, and *if* we have well-understood objectives, it should be relatively easy to specify just what impacts and effects the program is *supposed* to produce—but those can be two very big "if's.

This is where we go from the broad perspective to the gory details. Of all the things we had hoped for, what has happened? Equally important, what has happened that was *never* intended, and is it a good or a bad thing? How do we know whether something *is* a good or a bad thing, in the first place?

Unfortunately, most evaluations start and end only by looking at impacts and effects and they often do so in a very shallow fashion. The result is ignorance and complacency at worst and, at best, a few band-aid solutions slapped on over the cracks in the program. Impacts and effects should be looked at *after* you have diagnosed more fundamental problems of program mandate and objectives.

When we do look at impacts and effects, what questions can we ask? I think we first need to have some broad understanding of who the audience is and what it does. How many people participate in our theatre program? How many only watch? How many streak right on by? Who are they? Where are they from? How old are they?

What do they want from us? Do they like what we give them (whatever *that* means)? What do they come away with? What long-term effects does the program have?

Some of these are questions to which simple quantitative methods will provide some answers and will soothe, to some degree, senior management increasingly concerned about the high cost of educational theatre and what kind of "bang for the buck" it may be producing.

But we need to go further. We need to systematically examine, for every impact and effect the program is *supposed* to be producing, what is actually happening out there. If we are trying to produce learning, for example, it is *not* enough to stop at the affective level; there must be some attempt to get at the degree of cognitive learning that is taking place. This is where evaluation becomes extremely difficult.

A heritage institution, whatever its nature, is a buffet table, loaded with an array of learning opportunities and the bulk of our visitors saunter up to it, plates in hand, with widely varying tastes and degrees of hunger. What one takes away on one trip will likely be different, as to nature, quality, and quantity, from what one takes on another visit to the table. If each of our visitors is therefore learning different things, in different ways at different speeds and levels, how on earth can a single application of measurements capture all that learning?

This is why there is so little real evaluation of learning in heritage institutions.

4) ALTERNATIVES

The last question that evaluation asks is, Are there better ways of producing the desired results? In evaluating interpretation programs, this may mean several things. It may involve questioning the *kind or balance* of kinds of theatre that are going on. For example, it may suggest a move toward more scripted, or more interactive theatre, or a move to more (or less) single actor performances.

Sometimes, you may not even know the alternatives are there. A year or so ago, I was invited to do an informal peer review of live interpretation programs at a large and lively historic site, which is located in the middle of a small modern city. There is no way to control access to the site;

it merges unobtrusively with its surroundings. Accordingly, there has to be a staff member at the entrance to every building checking the visitor's pass. These people, known as visitor aides, are in costume and are generally highly knowledgeable individuals. One lady asked my companion and me which buildings we had already visited. I indicated the house of a colonial building contractor and mentioned how interesting an individual he must have been. "My, yes!" replied the interpreter, "he did so many things in this town. Why, he put the steeple and the addition on the parish church, on the other side of town, and he looked after the government buildings and he was very active in the community." She then talked about his wife and children, all the while quite unconsciously linking various parts of the site to each other and speaking as if she'd been there all the while. It was fascinating and was one of the relatively few types of live interpretation there that help the visitor link up the various bits and pieces, making it at least doubly valuable. When we described this experience to the interpretation managers at the site, they seemed surprised that this was going on.

Could this happen to you as well? Could there be a useful alternative right on your own site?

An evaluation may also suggest more mundane (but nonetheless useful) improvements to your program, involving scheduling, the relative length of performances, better locations, improvements for the comfort of visitors, etc.,—things that are related not only to the effectiveness of your live interpretation program, but to its *efficiency*, as well.

The ultimate "alternatives" question is, of course, Should the entire program be replaced with something better? It is not often, I must admit, that I have seen someone take his own program and place it on the block. However, unless you are willing to subject your program to searching, honest examination and produce the evidence to prove it works or the information that you can use to make it work, don't be surprised when your senior management takes the decision out of your hands and you find your actors replaced by a group of electronic kiosks—without really considering the consequences of such an action.

THE CASE STUDY

The theatre program at the Canadian Museum of Civilization was developed as part of the programming developed while the former National Museum of Man had been closed and the new Canadian Museum of Civilization was being constructed. The goals of the program were envisaged by the new museum's president to be:

- to attract increased visitation, particularly by persons who do not normally visit museums, through emphasizing entertaining and participatory qualities of live events over the traditionally passive educational museum experience;

- to generate revenues that will help support museum programmes for which the public is not charged; revenues may come directly through ticket sales or facility rentals, or indirectly through sales of events-related souvenirs and products created by artisans in demonstrations or again through increased expenditure in the museum's eateries;

- to enhance the visitor's museum experiences and increase intercultural understanding by using traditional and innovative theatrical techniques to make cultural heritage come alive;

- to attract media interest and coverage intended to stimulate increased public interest in, and visitation to, the museum;

- to create productions suitable for regional, national, or international distribution, especially by television or as audiovisual publications, and thereby to offer some of CMC's resources to all Canadians;

- to plan cooperative ventures with agencies, organizations, groups, and individuals, locally, regionally, and nationally; this will increase CMC's programming potential and visibility, foster community support, and give CMC greater opportunity to stimulate the performing arts in Canada; and

- to provide leadership for the Canadian museum community by developing and evaluating innovative techniques for live interpretation in a museum context.

Enormous cost overruns by the Crown corporation building the new museum, which, among other things, resulted in the museum opening with a large amount of unfinished space which is still under development, tempered the scope of the program actually put into place. Nonetheless, a brilliant and innovative program director, the late David Parry, was hired and developed a theatre company consisting of, by 1992 (the date of the evaluation), eight professional actors, a stage manager, and a dramaturge. Scripts, sets, and costumes were purchased under contract.

Two kinds of performances were provided in as many as eight locations in the museum's galleries—more than 30 playlets of 15-20 minutes duration covering specific topics such as 16th-century Basque whaling in the Gulf of St. Lawrence, and 13 first-person interactive performances by individual actors from a variety of periods in Canadian history, engaging visitors in open-ended dialogues.

Parry's approach was in the best tradition of Freeman Tilden. He saw three main objectives for the program:

1. Philosophical: Interpretive theatre in the museum should make audiences question everything they thought they knew about the human condition, allow them to feel comfortable about doing so, and leave them feeling that they have learned something quite new and been royally entertained in the process.

- to stimulate emotional and intellectual interest in and response to the museum's collections and exhibitsto provoke argument (but not to argue a point)to pose questions (but not to provide answers)to show what needs to be thought about (but not to state what needs to be done)

- to show that the interpretation of history and culture depend partly upon whose perspective you choose in the story you are telling

- to show that an artifact, a social interaction, or a transaction may have many meanings, some of which may not yet have occurred to anyone

- to show that some of these meanings may not yet have existed, and may perhaps not exist until some time in the future

- to explore and celebrate the similarities which join us in the human community, and the differences between us which make us fascinating to each other

- to reveal "the other" in ourselves, by showing the familiar in unfamiliar ways, and the unfamiliar in our own back yard

- to provoke laughter and tears, to excite, to startle, to shock, and occasionally to horrify the visitor, but above all to make sure that his or her visit is *never* ordinary

- to demonstrate and embody the idea that the experience the museum offers is immensely enjoyable, stimulating, and fun.

2. Informational: We *do* aim to provide information, but . . .[g]iving information . . . is not interpretation: "interpretation is revelation based on information, but the two are not the same."

3. Quality: "Since live interpretation and the performance mode are so integral to our new museum's mandate, exhibit orientation, and visitor appeal—and therefore ultimately to its economic viability—it is crucial that any theatrical interpretation we do be absolutely first-class. [Its existence] will make the visitor very interested, but also very critically aware . . . it must be good interpretation *and* good theatre."

In the summer of 1990, the museum commissioned a major exit survey, which was carried out by a major international research firm. It found that only 27 percent of the visitors claimed to have seen the theatrical program. The corporate president was incensed, in part because he had had such very high expectations for the program, but also because continuing resource limitations demanded that every program element should demonstrate success or perish. He was ready to terminate the program on the spot, but agreed to give it a stay of execution, pending the results of an evaluation. Suspicions that the survey may not have had very credible results (the questions on the theatre program came near the end of an exit survey of more than 60 items [!], when visitors were clearly exhausted not only from their visit [typically two to three hours in length] but also from answering such an extraordinarily long and boring questionnaire). The president also asked an outside agency—Parks Canada—to conduct a peer review. This was done very much as a "quick and dirty" exercise and the results provided no useful information to anyone.

First-person interpretation of the Canadian square timber trade of the 19th century by member of CMC theatre company in the timber shanty of the Museum's Canada Hall.. (Museum hostess at right.) *Photo by: Harry Foster/Steve Darby of Canadian Museum of Civilization.*

The evaluation could have been cut at several different levels, but, given that the very existence of the program was at stake, it was decided to conduct the kind of evaluation known as a program evaluation, which would examine all four of the basic issues set out above. We would challenge the program's mandate, assess its objectives and see how well they are being attained, examine the program's impacts and effects, and see what alternatives there might be for the program.

THE EVALUATION ASSESSMENT

We began by conducting what is known as an evaluation assessment, a planning study that describes the program and identifies its supposed mandate and objectives. It identifies the issues which could or should be addressed and the specific questions which must be asked to resolve these issues, as well as the methodologies that could be used to adduce the answers. More fundamentally, an evaluation assessment attempts to assess whether the program is even valuable and, if it is, is this the right time to do so. In our case, given the pressure from senior management, the last question was immaterial.

The evaluation assessment recommended that the evaluation address the following issues and attempt to answer their component questions:

1. Is the program's mandate appropriate? Are there better alternatives to the program? How essential is the interpretation program to the success of other CMC program components and of the museum as an institution?

1.1 Does the live interpretation program provide a museum service that cannot be delivered any other way?

1.2 How does the program support:
   • CMC's permanent and temporary galleries and exhibitions?
   • the less visible aspects of CMC's operations, such as educational programs, the National Postal Museum, etc.?
   • CMC's *overall* goals and objectives?

1.3 How essential is the program's contribution, viewed by:
   • other CMC programs?
   • CMC client groups?

1.4 What does the program contribute, relative to the costs required to maintain it?

1.5 How did use of the program's services affect the visitor's view of the value received for the cost of the museum visit?

1.6 Is there a better alternative for CMC to use to offer the required services?

1.7 Is there an appropriate mix and balance of program elements?

2.1 How much of the program's emphasis should be placed on:
   • first-person interpretation?
   • short vignettes related directly to particular gallery or exhibition elements?
   • productions related more generally to achieving the goals and objectives of CMC as a whole, such as those that build linkages among different galleries and exhibitions?

2.2 Should the kinds of interpretation offered and the relative balance among these vary according to the cyclical patterns of museum attendance?

2.3 Are there other services that the program should/could be offering, either:
   • in addition to current services? or,
   • instead of current services?

3. Is the program established and supported in such a way as to promote success?

3.1 What support services, at what levels, must be provided by other CMC elements to ensure the effectiveness of the live interpretation program?

3.2 Is the program adequately supported by such elements?

4. On what proportion of the visitor population(s) does the program impact?

4.1 How many members of which client groups observe/participate in the offerings of the program?

4.2 What factors influence their use of the program's services?

5. How does the program impact on CMC clients?

5.1 How did observation of/participation in the offerings of the program affect the museum experience of different kinds of clients?

5.2 What factors influenced the degree of impact or effect on different groups of clients?

5.3 Was the surprise of discovering such a program a factor in determining the success of individual museum visits?

5.4 How critical did different client groups view the program's contribution to the success of their individual museum experiences?

The evaluation assessment identified a number of methods through which the evaluation itself could be pursued. These included:
   • file reviews
   • unobtrusive observation
   • in-depth interviews
   • focus groups
   • surveys
   • peer review.

It must be admitted that, given the pressure to produce evaluative data with all possible speed, more time could and should have been taken to narrow down the questions to a more limited group of more precise questions.

Another flaw in the assessment was its recommendation that, because of the time constraints, it should be sole-sourced to a particular firm with experience in assessing live interpretation.

WHY WAS THIS A MISTAKE?

First, sole-sourcing puts the client rather at the mercy of the contractor, who generally feels that the client will have little choice but to accept what is offered as a product.

Second, and much more critical in this case, the assessment called for the kind of evaluation known in the trade as a program evaluation. While the contractor had considerable experience in assessing live interpretation, it became clear that the contractor had no experience whatever in conducting this depth of evaluation and the results were more superficial than had been hoped for. However, these are things that only became readily apparent in hindsight. The owl of Minerva invariably spreads its wings only with the coming of dusk!

THE EVALUATION AND ITS FINDINGS

We proceeded with the sole-source contract, confident that it would address the issues and ask the questions posited by the evaluation assessment. In retrospect, I was far too confident in the contractor, contrary to my usual policy.

The methods that were employed did not always follow the lines suggested in the assessment.

First, there were no focus groups. This was a major limitation because deep-seated feelings can often only be brought out in the context of a focus group—or through in-depth interviews with visitors, and there were none of these, either. Thus, we lost the only two methods that might have produced the most valuable information on the program's impacts on visitors.

There *were* adequate file reviews. Sufficient unobtrusive observation was conducted, especially in the early stages of the evaluation, as to more precisely target the methods that followed, and this, as Martha Stewart would have it, was "a good thing." Indeed, it made me realize even more than I had previously how absolutely essential it is to conduct unobtrusive observation during the planning stage of

almost any evaluation. It reveals so much that can help you make the most of your always limited evaluation resources.

The researchers and I agreed that mail-out and telephone surveys would not yield much information, but that an on-site survey was essential. This was very well handled by the consultant, who developed an ingenious sampling methodology which I commend to anyone wishing to study a theatre program. It is not enough to sample the participants at the end of a show; you have to look at those who (a) came early and left early; (b) came early and stayed for the entire performance; (c) came late and stayed for the entire performance, and (d) came late and left early. I was very much impressed by the quality of this particular method, and it yielded a lot of information from the 354 respondents interviewed—but, unfortunately, not very deep information.

There were a number of interviews conducted with managers and staff of related and supporting programs, enough, I think, to be able to assess the program in relationship to their corporate elements. There was not a real peer review, as it proved impossible to bring the peers together for a formal review exercise. Instead, they were contacted by telephone and the results were disappointing.

I should also say that program staff, including the actors, became very interested in the evaluation process and cooperated in every way. Yes, it is possible to argue that they knew their jobs were on the line, but their conduct during the evaluation revealed a very high degree of professionalism—and it became obvious as the evaluation progressed that the audiences appreciated it as much as management.

A real problem came in developing the report. I had a major row with the consultant, who insisted on my releasing the final payment on production of her draft report which was patently unacceptable in quality, though it was obvious to me that the research itself had been well done. As I refused to do so, this delayed production of the report for months and forced me to brief management on the strength of the draft report, which detracted from the credibility of the entire project. I must say that I had never, in more than 20 years of contracting for studies, encountered a contractor who insisted on receiving final payment on anything other than production of a final, acceptable report. However, I will admit to a share of the responsibility, as the contract had not been as specific as it might.

The draft report contained a great deal of useful information, as I have said, but it was not organized *at all* along the lines of the issues and questions identified by the assessment. After reviewing the text and making comments in great detail, providing pages of suggestions, and briefing the contractor's senior staff member for several hours, I had to accept a report which was very far from the program evaluation report I had expected. Moral of the story—make sure the shape of the product is clearly understood by the contractor *before* it is produced. I was particularly disappointed that there was no indication of which findings were supported by multiple lines of evidence and which by only one. As a result, all findings had to be treated with at least some care.

What did the study tell us? The following is the findings section of the actual report:

OVERALL SUMMARY OF RESULTS

The overall summary of results presents key issues and recurrent issues from the multi-method research design used to evaluate the CMC Live Interpretation Program. Results are sequenced in from the general to the specific and include results from all research methods, plus some results from one source only when the result is of particular importance to the program evaluation.

The use of live interpretation is growing in cultural institutions (both as a regular program and an intermittent program). It has been accepted into the repertoire of communication, interpretation and educational tools in many institutions. There is a growing body of knowledge concerning effective use of live interpretation and guidelines for success. Within the field, CMC is an important and active player.

At the time the program was developed, it was experimental.

The program achieved a lot in a very short period, and has been extremely productive.

The program is an established leader on the cutting edge of work in this field, both nationally and internationally.

First-person interpretation by member of the CMC theatre company in a temporary exhibition by the National Postal Museum (a component of CMC). *Photo by: Harry Foster/Steve Darby of Canadian Museum of Civilization.*

The majority of CMC staff interviewed view live interpretation as an essential activity. Almost all see opportunities for improvement both in the Live Interpretation Program as it exists and in the support it receives from other parts of the Museum. Most have already begun initiatives to improve the support they provide the Program.

Areas identified for internal and organizational improvements include:

- staff training and development in live interpretation and in planning
- infrastructure (live interpretation is spread across CMC)
- increasing efficiency and maximizing use of resources with respect to live interpretation.

Organizational support required for live interpretation includes:

- clear understanding of museum mission and how live interpretation relates to it
- organizational support from all functions involved (management, education, exhibitions, public relations, production, etc.)
- clear communication among staff involved with the program
- good support space (office, green room, dressing rooms, rehearsal, storage)
- planning for performance in exhibit spaces early on in the exhibit design process (as early as the first exhibit brief).

Reviewing all results. Especially the quantitative results of the visitors questionnaire, there were fewer differences between first person interactive performance and plays than expected. The results do reflect the fact that respondent groups remain intact during first person interactives, while they become part of a larger audience at plays.

More visitors attending first person interactive performances interact with other group members during the piece (45 percent, compared to 32 percent overall), and more stay and examine the exhibits following the piece (28 percent, compared to 16 percent overall). At plays, more visitors backtrack through exhibit areas they have already seen (34 percent, compared to 25 percent overall), and this occurs most frequently in the Tsimshian House where the exit is deliberately obscured.

As expected, more respondents attending first person interactives (59 percent) rated the level of interaction with the actors as very good than the respondents overall (47 percent).

More respondents at first person interactives were aware that they had learned something new from the performances (78 percent compared to 63 percent overall).

Visitors behave in different ways depending on the type of performance they are viewing and on the stage of the performance (pre-performance, during the performance, and post-performance).

Attendance varies greatly at all types of performances, and is influenced by five factors:
- overall attendance in the museum
- group dynamics among visitors
- time of arrival at performance—before or after the start
- the performance—type, content, and language
- performance area—size, proximity to major visitor paths, amenities.

The quality of performance areas in CMC varies greatly as a result of the following factors:
- space for the actors to arrive and prepare for the performance
- adequate space for the performance, including storage for props
- light levels
- sound penetration from other areas
- clear sight lines for viewers
- seating
- space for passersby
- mezzanines designed for comfortable viewing.

The vast majority of respondents, 95 percent (264), said that live interpretation *had enhanced their visit.* Respondents most frequently cited general and positive ways that live interpretation enhanced their visits (47 percent). This was closely followed by their feeling that live interpretation brought the museum, their visit, or history alive (45 percent) and to continue with live interpretation at CMC (27 percent).

The performance elicits a response in the vast majority, 90 percent, of visitors. The vast majority, 96 percent (242) of respondents felt they were entertained, while 63 percent (154) felt they had learned something new from the performance.

Professional actors are critical to visitor satisfaction of live interpretation at CMC. The actors and the acting were the factor of the performances that received the highest rating of all (4.6 out of a possible 5).

The most frequently cited reason visitors stayed at the piece (30 percent), the most liked aspect of the performance (43 percent), and the *Visitor orientation impacts on the effectiveness of the program:*

Time of arrival, or perceived time of arrival, influences whether or not visitors will stay and watch an entire performance.

The majority of viewers (89 percent) are not familiar with live interpretation at CMC.

The majority of viewers (86 percent) are not aware of the performance prior to their viewing it.

The strongest recommendations made by visitors were to provide more information on the existence of the program (34 percent).

The importance of providing effective orientation was also emphasized by CMC staff, by outside experts, and in the literature.

The least liked feature of the performance was the lack of comfort (32 percent). Specific reasons include the lack of seating, noise or poor sight lines in the performance area, and people entering and exiting during the performance.

The length of performances was just right for the majority, 85 percent (188), of respondents, too long for 12 percent (26), and too short for 4 percent (8). Experts have cited 10 minutes as a guideline for the maximum length of play.

The profile of visitors to live interpretation closely matches the CMC audience.

The majority of respondents (79 percent) are first-time visitors to CMC, and the primary reason cited for the visit was to see the exhibits in general (55 percent).

The majority of respondents (89 percent) are first-time viewers of live interpretation.

The majority of viewers sit in groups (90 percent), and most groups are made up of family members (67 percent); 42 percent of respondents in groups reported that children were included in their group.

Children in groups influence the decision to stay or leave live interpretation pieces, and a positive impact on children enhances the visit for adults. However, the impact of children in the group is lower than expected by some staff.

The majority of respondents influenced by group members reported that it was the children in their group who influenced the decision to stay (13 percent [20] compared to 15 percent overall) or leave (10 percent [9] compared to 16 percent overall).

However, this influence may not be as strong as the results above suggest: over twice as many respondents indicated that children had expressed a wish to stay (53) or a wish to leave (20).

Some (20) respondents cited that live interpretation enhanced their visit as a result of being positive for the children in their group.

There are more French-speaking respondents viewing live interpretation (40 percent) than are found in the CMC audience overall (20 percent).

Language is an important factor in a visitor's decision whether or not to stay and view a performance; however, visitors routinely stay to watch a performance in their second official language. The decision is based on the visitor's ability to understand the language of the performance.

The second most common reason for not staying was lack of understanding of the language of the piece (25 percent).

Among the 15 (16 percent) respondents who cited language as the least-liked feature, 10 visitors specified not understanding the language of the piece.

Bilingualism in pieces is viewed positively more often than negatively.

Among the 22 respondents citing language as a most-liked feature, 15 mentioned bilingualism specifically.

Among the 15 respondents who cited language as the least-liked feature, only 2 mentioned bilingualism.

While the report did not follow the organization suggested by the issues identified in the assessment, it is clear that most of the questions were answered and that the issues had been addressed.

The report then went on to make literally dozens of recommendations for improving not only the program itself, but for changes in corporate policy and the activities of related programs to better integrate live interpretation with the programs it was intended to extend and support. As a planning document, it was extremely helpful for both management and staff.

Interestingly, the study had the unexpected result of turning some of the most senior managers who had formerly sneered at the program into staunch supporters—which helps to explain the success of implementing the recommendations.

In the six years since the study was conducted, efforts have been made to carry out as many of the recommendations as possible. Regrettably, the report was presented at the beginning of a multi-year program of cutbacks and retrenchment, which severely limited what could be done, but this takes nothing away from the study's effectiveness.

CONCLUSION

It was a learning experience for all who participated in the project, including myself, all the more so as, from what we could gather, no one had previously attempted such a program evaluation.

Could we have achieved the same results without employing the program evaluation approach? I doubt it. Educational theatre programs are difficult to evaluate. I believe that only the framework and methodological discipline imposed by the framework of program level evaluation can ensure an evaluation that will give one adequate direction to improve not only the program but those to which it is linked and that will, at the same time, have the credibility to stand up to the searching gaze of corporate management.

BIBLIOGRAPHY

There have been few evaluations conducted of live interpretation and very few indeed of museum theatre programs, so an extensive bibliography does not exist. The citations that follow consist of selected references on:
• initiating museum evaluation and visitor studies programs
• program evaluation
• evaluating learning in museums, especially within the context of family groups, and
• measuring museum effectiveness.

A comprehensive international bibliography can be downloaded from the Canadian War Museum Web site, at: http://www.civilization.ca/cwm. A "searchable" version of this Web site will be offered shortly by the Museum Studies Program of the University of Toronto, on its Web site.

Ambrose, T. M., "Forward Planning for Museums and the Setting of Performance Standards," in: Boxer, G., G. Kilminster and T. Ambrose (Eds.), Measuring the Immeasurable. 1994: 30-33.

Anderson, P. and Roe, B. C. 1993. *The Museum Impact and Evaluation Study: Roles of Affect in the Museum Visit and Ways of Assessing Them* (summary). Chicago: Museum of Science and Industry.

Bicknell, Sandra and Xerxes Mazda. 1993. "Enlightening or embarrassing: an evaluation of drama in the Science Museum." London: National Museum of Science and Industry.

Bitgood, Stephen, Benefeld & Patterson (Eds.) *Visitor Studies: Theory, Research and Practice* (Proceedings of annual conferences, 1988-1996), Jacksonville, Ala.: Center for Social Design, 1989-97.

Blud, L.M. (1990). "Social Interaction and Learning Among Family Groups Visiting a Museum", *Museum Management and Curatorship* 9 (1): 43-51.

Borun, M., A. Cleghorn & C. Garfield, "Family Learning in Museums: A Bibliographic Review," Curator 38/4, 1995: 262-270.

\Bud, R., M. Cave and S. Hanney, "Measuring a Museum's Output," *Museums Journal* 91/1, 1991: 29-31.

Fitz-Gibbon, Carol T., *How to Design a Program Evaluation*, Sage Publications, 1987.

Hein, G. E., "Evaluation of museum programmes and exhibits," in: Hooper-Greenhill, E. (Ed.), *The Educational Role of the Museum*. (Leicester Readers in Museum Studies). London/New York, 1994: 306-312.

Hein, G. E. and Engel, B. S. 1981. 'Qualitative Evaluation of Cultural Institution/School Education Programs," in S. N. Lehman and K. Inge (Eds.) *Museum-School Partnerships: Plans and Programs*. Washington, DC: Center for Museum Education.

Jackson, J. M:, "The Measurement of Museums' Performance," in: Boxer, G., G. Kilminster & T. Ambrose (Eds.), *Measuring the Immeasurable*. 1994: 5-20.

Jackson, P. M. (1991), "Performance indicators: promises and pitfalls," in: Moore, K. (Ed.), *Museum Management*. (Leicester Readers in Museum Studies). London/New York, 1994: 156-172.

Korn, Randi, Susan Ades, and Conny Graft, "Evaluation of an Experimental Interpretive Program," *History News*, Nashville, Tenn.: 50 (4), 1995: 19-24.

Miller, D. Stuart. "The Effect of Interpretive Theatre on Children in the Museum Setting." Georgia Southern College: thesis, 1988.

Morganstern, D. (1996). "The Sociocultural Impact of Portraying the Past: Old Tucson and Plimoth Plantation," Bitgood, S.C. (Ed.) (1996). *Visitor Studies: Theory, Research, and Practice*. Vol. 7, Issue 1. Jacksonville, Ala.: Visitor Studies Association. Selected Papers from the 1994 Visitor Studies Conference: 88-98.

Mullins, G. W., "Understanding interpretive clientele," *Visitor Behavior* VI/2, 1991: 5-6.

Munley, Mary Ellen. reprinted 1993. "Buyin' Freedom." *Perspectives on Museum Theatre*. Washington, D.C.: American Association of Museums: 69-94.

Needham, Harry, "Improving Live Interpretation Programs Through Evaluation," in J.-M. Blais (Ed.) *Les langages de l'interprétation personnalisée: L'animation dans les musées/ The Languages of Live Interpretation: Animation in Museums*, Hull (Québec): Canadian Museum of Civilization, 1997, pp. 161 - 168.

Needham, Harry, "Evaluating Live Interpretation Programs," *Evaluation and Visitor Research in Museums*: 'Towards 2000 Conference Papers' March 1995, Sydney: Powerhouse Museum, 1996, pp. 139-153.

Needham, Harry, "Measuring Client Satisfaction and Integrating it into the Performance Equation," (paper presented to the conference Effectively Measuring & Evaluating Government Programs & Operations, Ottawa, 27-28 February 1997), [to be published by Insight Information Inc., Toronto].

Needham, Harry, "Using Program Evaluation to Improve Live Interpretation," paper presented to the 1995 Visitor Studies Conference, St. Paul, Minn., published in *Visitor Studies: Theory, Research and Practice*, Vol.8, Jacksonville Ala.: Visitor Studies Association, 1996.

Needham, Harry, "Wisdom, Interpretation and the Public: Is the Gap Closing or Opening Even Further?" (keynote address) abstract in proceedings of the Fourth Annual Interpretation Association of Australia Conference, Canberra, 13-15 November 1995.

Roggenbuck, J. W. & D. B. Propst, "Evaluation of Interpretation," in: University of Victoria (Ed.), *Introduction to Museums Studies* III. Victoria, B. C., 1985.

Screven, C. G., *The measurement and facilitation of learning in the museum environment: An experimental analysis*. Washington D. C. 1974.

Serrell, B. (1991). "Learning Styles and Museum Visitors," *ILVS Review: A Journal of Visitor Behavior* 2 (1): 137-139.

RESPONSE TO *Evaluation of Theatre: Evaluation Is a Must!*

GEORGE E. HEIN, SENIOR RESEARCH ASSOCIATE
PROGRAM EVALUATION AND RESEARCH GROUP, LESLEY COLLEGE

Harry Needham's provocative chapter can be neatly divided into two parts: a general perspective on evaluation and a detailed case study. Each section has strengths and limitations.

Needham makes a powerful argument for using evaluation as a management tool to review the place of museum theater in the museum's overall mission. He argues that museum staff should go beyond technical evaluations—finding out who your visitors are (demographic studies), how visitors use a program, and how satisfied they are with it—and undertake the more valuable, "deeper" effort to answer the question, "How can an evaluation be used to provide (or disprove) the effectiveness of [educational theater] programs—and their indispensability?" For this task, he urges the use of program evaluation, defined as a four-level activity examining the mandate of a program, whether its objectives are being met, what the impact of the program is, and whether the particular program represents the best way to achieve these goals.

These are powerful questions and valuable for any museum to address in a program evaluation. They are also challenging questions and will involve staff in intense introspection and, probably, in serious debates about the allocation of resources, staff responsibilities, and institutional mission. Museum staff need to recognize that the decision to carry out such a sweeping program evaluation will involve a major commitment from all levels of museum personnel and engage them in an examination of their basic beliefs and goals.

Many actual evaluations of museum theater programs are necessarily more modest, asking only whether the particular play or first person interpretation activity enhances a specific exhibition or whether it is comprehensible to the audience it attracts. Although grand institutional evaluations can be powerful, they are not appropriate for every situation. Also, the details of how to carry out either major program evaluation or more limited technical evaluations, and the resources required, are not addressed in this chapter.

The second section, a case study of the program evaluation of the theater program at the Canadian Museum of Civilization, illustrates some of the issues that are likely to arise in carrying out a major program evaluation. Unfortunately, its value is limited because it provides enormous detail on some aspects of the story and slights other components. Needham provides a long set of program goals, but only a brief summary of the theater program itself, so that the long excerpt from the evaluation report's conclusions is difficult to interpret. Also, a staggering, comprehensive set of evaluation questions is paired with only a brief mention of the evaluation means used. One of the crucial components of any evaluation, large or small, is the matching of ways to gather data (questionnaires, interviews, observations, unobtrusive measures, visitor drawings, delayed interviews, etc.) and the timing of this field work with the evaluation issues. Concerned readers will find only hints to assist them in thinking about how to select appropriate evaluation means to address particular evaluation questions. Finally, the focus on the unique problems encountered in this case study with a sole-source contractor obscures the more general issues of matching any evaluator's style and work methods with institutional needs and expectations.

The chapter provides a strong message that evaluation of any program is essential and that it can provide a major contribution to overarching institutional questions about interpretation, when carried out on a grand scale. Some of the problems in hiring outside evaluators are also spelled out. For readers who want practical advice on how to actually do evaluation of their own theater programs, or who are limited to more modest efforts, the references may be more useful than the detailed case study.

CHAPTER 12

THE FUTURE OF MUSEUM THEATER
THE PLAY'S THE THING!

Christy S. Matthews, Director of Operations, Colonial Williamsburg

*A murmur of voices echoes throughout the large and impos-
ing room. The Royal Governor and his Council ready themselves for the business of this court. Curious onlookers peer
through the doorways of the side rooms, wondering which will
reveal Grace Sherwood. Witnesses huddle together with fierce
resolve despite the fact that abject fear is apparent on their
faces. Suddenly, a large, creaking door opens and an immediate silence befalls the space. The silence is broken not by voices,
but by the heavy iron chains that scrape and pound against
the wooden floor. The constable leads a slight, attractive
woman by the arm while she struggles to walk with her wrists
and ankles chained. She stands before the Council ready to
face those who have accused her of being a witch.*

The event described above plays out three to four nights a
week at Colonial Williamsburg. The program called *Cry
Witch*! is a trial recreation of the only known allegation of
witchcraft in Virginia. The audience is enraptured from
the beginning. They are active participants in the proceedings. Many serve as justices who must decide Grace
Sherwood's fate based on law, not opinion. Others squirm
at the testimonies and subsequent legal definitions and
tests she must perform to prove her guilt or innocence.
Once the verdict is handed down, the audience readily
makes its sentiment known. This play and the inter-
preter-led discussion with the audience at its conclusion,
teach complex issues and attitudes of early 18th-century
Virginia. In addition to the lessons on the legal process, the
audience explores roles of women, concepts of faith and
intellectualism, and cultural differences between north-
ern and southern colonies. All of this information is con-
veyed in one hour! And the audience gets it.

WHERE WE'VE BEEN

Cry Witch! is one of many educational programs at
Colonial Williamsburg that uses various theatrical techniques to reach and teach its diverse audience. The reason
is clear. Theater is an art form that essentially imitates

varying aspects of life. This allows us to feel, excites all of
our senses, and most importantly, makes us care.
Educators know instinctively that students, regardless of
age, will learn more when they care about the subject presented. For these reasons, in the last 40 years, many outdoor or living history museums throughout the United
States have used various forms of theater as an integral
part of public programming. These museums often refer
to their theatrical programs as "people of the past,"
"re-enactors" or "first person." Some use scripted works,
but most rely on the knowledge and improvisational skill
of staff members. There are also a few museums that
have theater of different time periods as a subject of study
and presentation.

About 25 years ago, the Science Museum of Minnesota
became the first science museum in the United States to
incorporate theater as a part of its educational program.
The use of theater in other traditional museums has followed. The programs cleverly incorporate music, dance,
puppetry, or character portrayals to introduce subjects like
astronomy, conservation, and paleontology. For example,
the New Mexico Museum of Natural History offered a
puppet program called *Antarctica Nightly News*. Using a
talk-show format familiar to both parents and children,
penguins introduced different guests (a variety of Antarctic
species), which allowed them to discuss issues important to
each. In recent years, science museums have focused
shows at more mature audiences. The Museum of Science
in Boston offers *Mapping the Soul*, a powerful and highly
effective piece that informs audiences of the potential
social, ethical, and legal implications of the Human
Genome Project. Art museums and other disciplines have
also incorporated theater into their programming.

STILL NEED TO PROVE ITS POWER

Although these and other museums have highly successful programs, hurdles remain in sustaining and in initiat-

ing more museum theater. Skeptical museum directors and governing boards still request data that supports the educational benefit, cost efficiency, or audience-building potential of this innovative medium. Some curators continue to oppose museum theater adamantly because of its inherent extrapolation of known facts. They fear misinformation and misunderstanding. Those in the museum theater field need to educate their museum colleagues. These questions and issues have led a few practitioners to gather quantifiable data on visitor reaction, knowledge retention and audience diversification, but not enough. Although there is increased interest, the research is still relatively scant and most of the available information remains anecdotal. Despite these seeming limitations, the field continues to grow. However, in order to secure a hold in museums, we must ask ourselves what the future of museum theater will be?

TWO CAMPS OF MUSEUM THEATER

The answer lies in how well a number of important issues are addressed in the next few years. The issues generally fall into two categories: philosophy and application. While rarely explicitly stated, it seems two distinct camps have emerged over the years: the historic site museum and museums of art, science, or technology, along with zoos and aquariums (traditional museums). These two camps use different styles of theater, which has led to some disagreement in philosophy. When each begins exploring how to apply theater, it becomes a much easier dialogue since there are several models across the spectrum of institutions. Reaching consensus on philosophy seems possible, but what often impedes the dialogue is the language that each uses: actors vs. interpreters, living history vs. theater, etc. These semantic differences create an air of suspicion between the camps. Another sensitive point is that there are those on both sides who have suggested setting guidelines that define and recognize good museum theater, much in the same way a museum gets accredited. In order to do that, a new common language needs to be introduced.

One primary difference is that historic sites rarely refer to their staff as actors, but rather as interpreters. The reasons for the term "interpreter" are that the performer is required to know a great deal of historical information beyond a set script and to develop the skills appropriate to

the characters portrayed beyond those illustrated within a play. Historic sites also use informal music and dance to help create a sense of the past. Character portrayals and re-enactment of past events shape these programs. In recent years, many in historic sites feel their work has been slighted by the traditional museum group, because of this reliance on character portrayals and reenactments, which are rarely scripted. The chasm has widened when historic sites perceive that scripted character portrayals offered in traditional museums are touted as new and innovative. Historic site staff criticize traditional museums for what they consider a lack of care in costuming and academic preparation of the actors that can make for performances that are shallow, especially with character portrayals.

While some in the traditional museum group have perceived re-enactments at historic sites as merely a *fait accompli* for demonstration purposes, historic site staff do not. Rather, they consider re-enactments of historical events to be full-fledged theater and resist the notion that the lack of formal theatrical training of most historic-site staff makes their performances weak and ill-conceived. Lastly, there has been a misconception that historic sites offer a limited range of theatrical programming compared to what is offered at traditional museums, which is not necessarily the case. Fortunately, a number of professionals from both camps have started a dialogue that is finally beginning to break down these barriers.

As the dialogue progresses, it has become abundantly clear that each really is defining and applying standards to museum theater in much the same way. The only apparent difference is that historic sites use their museum as the stage and set, while most traditional museums use auditoriums or specially designed exhibition spaces as the performance space. They each recognize the importance of training and creating appropriate settings. Each wants to provide an experience for the museum visitor that is thoughtful, creative, educational, and relevant. Most importantly, each recognizes how theatrical techniques if done well can create a lasting and meaningful impression on its audiences.

NEED FOR NETWORKING

In the past, there have been workshops and conference sessions offered to share information on museum theater. However, if the field is to continue to move forward professional organizations such as the National Association of Interpreters (NAI), the American Association for State and Local History (AASLH), AAM's Museum Theater Professional Interest Council, and the International Museum Theater Alliance (IMTAL) should collaborate on a national level to provide training opportunities, round table discussions, and showcase different museum theater programs. To date, it has been a difficult financial and planning prospect for any one organization. A collective effort would provide valuable information and resources that could benefit everyone.

HOW TO PROCEED

When any institution decides to add museum theater to its offerings, there are a number of important questions that must be considered:

- If data supports it, how does the museum ensure its theater program is viewed as integral versus add-on?

- Should the museum work with a local theater group or hire its own actors? If you work with a theater group, what are some best practices for collaboration?

- Should museums work with the academic community to update curricula for new museum professionals that incorporates skills to manage theater programs in a museum setting?

- Is there a need to work with other organizations to develop training programs for playwrights, directors, and performers?

- Should the actor's, director's, or playwright's work in a museum setting be considered as fulfilling the requirements of their respective unions?

- How do we begin to clarify intellectual property and subsequent copyright issues?

PLAN FIRST

Currently, when a museum curator considers adding a theater component to public programming, he or she starts making a series of phone calls trying to contact anyone in their region who may have experience with this kind of programming. In the future, the curator will simply set the exhibition objectives, identify the audiences that the institution wants to reach, and begin work on all the programming elements. This may seem like a simple notion on the surface, but the reality is that a number of institutions decide *after* the exhibition has been planned to add a theater element. In order for the field to continue to advance, museum professionals have to move beyond this practice. Failure is imminent if they do not. Such was the story of a colleague in the Midwest.

Newly appointed to her post, she was excited about the opportunity to develop a variety of programs that she felt would be relevant to the community that her museum served. After a few months, I received a frantic call from her. It seemed as though her director wanted her to develop a theater program for an upcoming exhibition. The problem was that he was giving her six weeks to get it up and running. She did not have any scripts to work with, actors had never been involved with the museum before, and she knew no one in the small theater community in her area. To make matters worse, she wasn't entirely sure where this performance was actually going to take place. Why didn't she tell him it can't be done? There were probably a lot of reasons, but more likely than not, she viewed this as her opportunity to prove that museum theater could be an exciting addition to her museum's public programming.

After much discussion, she came up with a model that I thought might work and help her save face if the whole thing fell apart! But she had to work fast. Her first order of business was to call the local theater group and find out who were the major players, and then who really had the talent. She then contacted the university about 40 miles away to see if there were any students who might be interested in writing and performing the piece. They developed it by doing a series of improvisational exercises in their classes. It was agreed that the script that they developed would be the property of the principal student writers. In the meantime, she started running advertisements in the regional newspapers about this wonderful, experimental museum program that would provide big laughs for all ages. While the script could have been reworked, the overall premise was quite clever.

The play starts with a group of students that have to run the local museum in order to save the town from aliens who think nothing on earth, let alone anything produced by humans, is worth saving. To make matters worse, none of the students knows anything about all the different jobs in the museum. The students do everything wrong, like leaving a priceless lamp in an unsecured area, and it gets stolen. Another tries to wipe a cola spill off a painting and ruins it, and so on. When all was said and done, the play had nothing to do with the exhibition, but everything to do with building audience appreciation for the museum's collection and preservation efforts. The show ran for two weekends and was ruled a failure because the program only drew about fifty audience members per performance! The failure was not the show, but rather her director who presumed that a program could be put together so quickly, with little to no institutional support. That director would have never walked into the curator's office and demanded an exhibition in that kind of time with so little support. Yet he was willing to do this to the theater program. Again, in order for museum theater to advance, we must think of its role as integral to the institution.

A colleague in the South cringed when I shared that story. He felt immune to that kind of problem because he had a director who was very supportive of museum theater. The director had personally investigated other programs around the country and was wildly optimistic about the possibilities. The museum was slated to open a major new exhibition. The educator was involved in the planning from the beginning. He was given a generous budget to hire a playwright and theater director as well as provide great pay for the actors. They all worked hand in hand with the curatorial and public relations staff to make the theater aspect of the exhibit just as important as its installation. The program idea was that at several points throughout the exhibit, audiences would encounter dramatic and comedic scenes, as well as interactive character portrayals. What could possibly have gone wrong?

FIND THE BALANCE

The balance in the exhibition was lost. The exhibition was difficult to follow when the actors were not on site, which was often. After the exhibit was up for about four months, actors started leaving the show because many of them grew weary of the tedious regimen. Their schedule required them to do performances every fifteen to twenty minutes in two hour intervals with half hour breaks in between. Another problem was that there were too many

actors throughout the exhibition. With each one doing six to eight minute pieces, they discovered that the audience did everything they could to avoid any section were they heard an actor around the corner. This audience flight was happening before they got half way through the exhibit! So, the museum decided to cut back on the number of actors. That decision made the exhibit even more exasperating for the audience. It did not take long for the exhibit to be labeled a failure. What's the point? There is a balance that must be maintained. Museum theater does not work in every setting. More importantly, the museum program must not be more ambitious than the exhibition it's ultimately designed to support. That's right, support. That is the function of museum theater. If it were more than that, then you are running a theater, not a museum. As more proponents become attuned to these realities, the more likely they are to have the kind of impact they desire.

A DREAM OF MUSEUM THEATER

So where do we go from here? Let's dream of the perfect world, somewhere in the not too distant future. Imagine that you are a small museum that wants to incorporate a theater program into an upcoming exhibition. You make one call and get a list of several museum and theater professionals in your area. You arrange a meeting between the museum's key personnel and the consultant group to explore the creative possibilities based on your budget. They also provide sample contracts that let you decide if all rights to the work will be maintained by the museum or be shared with the writer. You also get a list of writers, directors, and actors who provide the services you need. You make a few more calls to find out who is available. After careful deliberation, you choose a writer with experience writing for children. The writer also agrees to relinquish all rights to the museum. The writer then gets assigned to a curator who provides all the technical information about the subject of the exhibition. The writer understands that there will be minimal sets and simple black costumes for the actors. In the meantime, you begin notifying the community that actors are being sought for a special children's program being planned at the museum. You have found a director to handle the audition, choose the actors, and plan the rehearsal schedules.

After careful planning, you arrange for previews at local churches and schools. You initiate a discount program that will get the child into the museum free for every adult fee. The entire town is buzzing about this new thing at the museum. The exhibit and show will run one evening during the week and once on the weekend. Since your community is relatively small, you decide to run the program for six weeks, and mount another for six more weeks, since you are dependent on repeat community audiences. Your exhibit opens, and children arrive with their parents in tow. The program is a delightful introduction to the exhibit that lasts about twenty minutes. At its conclusion, excited children enter the exhibit area to complete their adventure. Meanwhile, adult audiences are given the option of moving through the exhibit to make discoveries of their own. After each finishes the exhibit, they are greeted by a docent who asks audiences a few questions about their experience. When the museum closes for the day and counts its receipts, they all realize that the modest increase in ticket sales help cover the expense of the program. As the exhibit continues its run, the percentage of return visitors increases as does audience satisfaction with their museum experience. The young museum steadily gains a reputation as a place where families can gather for fulfilling experiences.

How far from this dream are we? Remarkably, not too far. A number of organizations that support museum theater have compiled lists of institutions and individuals that can assist in the development of programs. However, the lists are incomplete. At best, 50 institutions and perhaps 400 individual members belong to these groups combined. However, these numbers to do not reflect the amount of work actually being done. There are a number of museums out there that offer creative programming that incorporates puppetry, dance, or theater in their public programming. Most of them don't know that there are organizations to assist them. Additionally, many of these institutions do not think their efforts would qualify them for membership in museum theater interest groups. To rectify this problem, networking efforts need to be intensified. There is also a need for a continued presence at conferences and announcements for museum professionals to help spread the word.

MUSEUM THEATER TRAINING

Most museum professionals did not enter the field with a degree in museum studies. While there are a number of museum studies programs around the country, only a few actually offer courses that devote time to theater in museums. The closest course work offered falls under arts management. So how do we train our colleagues? As suggested earlier, the time has come to develop a series of extended workshops. It may even be possible to establish a certification program at some of the premier universities that offer museum studies programs. This suggestion is not as far-fetched as you may think. At the University of Pittsburgh, efforts are under way to develop a series of courses in the theater department that trains students in writing, direction, and performance in a museum setting. Conversations have been ongoing at the College of William and Mary and Hampton University (both in Virginia) to develop similar programs in the theater and museum studies departments. Bretton Hall in England has offered a museum theater undergraduate course. The next five years will be important in determining whether or not these are worthwhile efforts.

FORM ALLIANCES

In the meantime, we can begin to invite members of the local theater community to our museums and begin forming alliances. This is important whether or not you decide to hire your own staff of performers. Realistically, most museums cannot afford to have a full-time staff. At best, a museum may have a theater coordinator. Therefore, it makes more sense to get help from outside your institution, especially since most museum programs are 30 minutes or less. Offer your institution as a training ground for aspiring writers and directors. What is their incentive to form an alliance with you? Few theaters, let alone museums, know that Actor's Equity (the theater union) has begun to recognize the work at museums, and has agreed to give qualifying credits for union membership to museum theater actors. Two years ago, Colonial Williamsburg entered into discussion with Equity about how one of its employees might get Equity credit for their work. Equity made the decision to consider museum theater work as it does amusement park entertainment. (By all means, do not take offense to that!). Though there are still some restrictions, this is very good incentive for young performers. The Writer's Guild is less restrictive for playwrights. Their rules allow for work done for museums as long as it is a public performance. How many credits a writer earns is based on the length of a particular work.

Few community theaters meet the criteria that would permit their performers to get these kinds of creative credits with the unions. This can be an incredible selling point in encouraging theater people to get involved with your museum. Use it.

Lastly, our future depends on who owns the work we do. When our institutions install an exhibition and publish a guide to the collection, we own everything. So why would we give away rights to an outside writer? If at all possible, establish a work-for-hire arrangement with the writer that turns over all rights to the museum. Some museums share the rights, which can be a very beneficial arrangement. However, if you do this, make sure that you have a say in what venues the show is presented, that appropriate credit is given to your museum, and if there will be royalties paid to use it. These suggestions may be contrary to the practices of the theater world, but remember museum theater is a hybrid. If you play your cards right, writers will come to you with ideas and offers.

Museum theater has been with us for a long time. There seems to be very little need for a bureaucratic accreditation process. It is simple enough to call a few colleagues and invite them in to critique your work. By being open and constructive with one another and sharing in successes, we can move the quality of our work forward. Theater is an art form that constantly reinvents itself while hanging on to the very principles that make it strong. The same can and should be said of museums. We can appeal to diverse audiences, we can educate, and we always hope to inspire people. There is little doubt that museum theater is here to stay, and its future is as bright as its strongest advocates.

AUTHOR'S NOTE:

While I am comfortable identifying museums that have done well, I have refrained from identifying those whose work is questionable, at best. Therefore, the genders of colleagues may have been switched or they have been located in different regions of the country. What is important here is the lesson that these stories provide. I assure you that each story depicted is true, only the names have changed to protect the not so innocent!

RESPONSE TO *The Future of Museum Theater—Future Challenges*

LAURA MALONEY AND CATHERINE HUGHES

The use of story and performance to share tales of times past has been around for as long as there were humans. We are still drawn to drama today—whether that be via a Broadway play, a town playhouse, motion picture, television show, or a child's school room where they enact stories of importance or those that are just plain fun. Drama is an essential part of our human heritage.

Theater is a natural tool for teaching others about our world. It allows us to laugh, cry, challenge, wonder, and dream. It can be very forceful or quite subtle in its approach.

Consequently, it makes sense that historical organizations like Colonial Williamsburg have been using it as a central means for communicating for at least 40 years. Yet, only 25 years ago did a formal theater program emerge in a more traditional museum at the Science Museum of Minnesota. Why did it take so long for museums and other organizations to begin to adopt this age-old form of entertainment and education? Is it the unpredictability of live performance? The cost? Fear of less-than-accurate interpretation? It seems the answer is, a little bit of all of these, plus a few more we haven't mentioned. Furthermore, are these questions still holding the museum theater field back?

ISSUES FACING THEATER

LACK OF UNDERSTANDING AMONG DIRECTORS, GOVERNING BOARDS, AND CURATORS

Educators have long struggled with the fact that they're among the last to be included in the exhibit design process. Such poor planning can lead to ill-conceived concepts and poorly produced programs. Education programs are often considered an easy add-on. Since theater is most often aligned with museum education departments, it is understandable that it, too, would be faced with some of the same problems faced by traditional educators.

In our experience, directors have understood theater to be relatively easy to produce with few resources. Finding a way to educate our directors and curators about what goes into producing successful theater will be helpful in addressing these kinds of management issues, which will ultimately improve the quality of our programming.

NEED FOR QUANTITATIVE DATA TO CONVINCE THE SKEPTICS

Christy addressed the all-too-common problem of curators opposing theater due to a fear of misinterpretation of the facts. This appears to affect all museums, zoos, and aquariums, particularly in relation to the disciplines of history and science. Their grip, however, appears to be loosening at a significant rate.

There may be a few reasons for greater acceptance among the skeptics. First, those working in the museum theater field are learning how to better design and implement programs. Also, several of us are turning to professionals for either advice and/or talent. Second, there is a bit more research being done on theater's effectiveness, though more needs to be done.

INTELLECTUAL PROPERTY AND COPYRIGHT

The copyright issue is a growing one within our field. Both sides are used to having complete creative and practical control, which has produced some difficult negotiations. Shared copyright seems logical for many institutions, but IMTAL needs to collect more information from the field and disseminate successful models.

SEPARATE CAMPS BUILD OPPOSITION VERSUS UNIFICATION

There is still some disparity among practicing museum theater professionals about the language of theater. We are also struggling with how theater is defined. We need to continue to answer the question: what is museum theater? Rather than use the answers for exclusion, we need to see the many answers as a way to expand the definition. There is no room for ownership or power struggles for the term. This will divide us. Instead, the arguments over definition must turn into a discussion of quality.

THE FUTURE

In the next few years, we expect to see rapid growth within the museum theater field. We agree with Christy that the following issues will receive the greatest attention over the next few years.

1. INCREASED COLLABORATION

As more and more institutions turn to theater as a tool for education, our need for networking increases. Exploring various perspectives exponentially multiplies our learning. This publication is a result of such networking. We hope this work will breed new projects that set out to resolve or discuss issues affecting us all.

As Christy noted, forming alliances with local theater groups or universities may be an effective approach in developing a program. They may assist museums, zoos, and aquariums in a few ways. First, the program may be more strongly supported by the community. Second, such partnerships may assist in reducing the financial burden of developing and launching a theater program, as students may exchange performance for credit or a community acting troupe may volunteer for special events. There are myriad possibilities.

2. NEED FOR A UNIFIED VOICE

Although there are several budding advisory or theater networking groups, we still lack a strong voice. Without a strong and unified presence, we lack the power to make swift industry changes. Every association meeting (AZA, AAM, NAI, AASLH, etc.) should hold a session to discuss opinions, problems, and solutions. With a focused effort we will be better equipped to handle the challenges of effectively managing a museum theater program while enthusiastically greeting newcomers.

3. MORE RESEARCH

As with any business, statistics are needed to convince our leaders that an expenditure or investment is worthwhile. The greater our effectiveness (according to the statistics), the more likely it is that funds will be shifted to our programs. Additionally, evaluation and research will:

- Keep us honest and focused on improvement.
- Provide a solid foundation of support when seeking outside funding.
- Provide us with the information needed to sway the skeptics.

Some directors will require proof that theater works before allocating resources to it. And, in the face of budget cuts, programs already in existence may have to prove that their program adds significant value to the visitor experience. Credible research and evaluation can provide us with this information.

4. STANDARDIZATION

We must beware that to come to any consensus on qualifying factors for excellence in museum theater risks limiting what it might be. However, as we continue to discuss and define "good museum theater," we will begin developing a loose set of guidelines from which to work. The key to our success will be standardizing without sacrificing our individuality.

5. OWNERSHIP ISSUES

As discussed earlier, the field is now sorting through the issue of copyrights. We do not expect this to be resolved overnight as the two industries—theater and museum—work together. We do hope that a fair and equal agreement for all is reached.

As we push forward into the new millennium, we face many exciting challenges. The issues discussed in this publication are just a small fraction of those with which we all have been, and will be, dealing. Progress continues. Just 25 ago, the Science Museum of Minnesota began a theater program within a museum. Twenty-five years from now we hope to have advanced significantly to the point where museum theater is a thoroughly integrated, ever-dynamic presence throughout our institutions.

APPENDIX A

INTERNATIONAL MUSEUM THEATRE ALLIANCE
(IMTAL)

Promoting theatre as effective education for museums, zoos and aquaria
IMTAL website: www.mos.org/IMTAL
email: imtal@mos.org

WHAT IS IMTAL?

IT'S A PROFESSIONAL RESOURCE!

The International Museum Theatre Alliance [IMTAL], formed in 1990, is a professional resource and networking non-profit organization for museum and theatre professionals using theatre as an interpretive technique. Membership to the Alliance is open to professionals using all styles and techniques of this expanding medium.

IT'S A COMMUNICATION NETWORK!

In 1994, IMTAL became the Affiliate Group on Museum Theatre for the American Association of Museums. Through this relationship, and with associate members, such as Heritage Interpretation International, IMTAL advocates for museum theatre, exchanging and dissemination information.

The Alliance serves as a forum for developments, debate and opportunities in museum theatre.

IT'S FOR EVERYONE!

IMTAL is composed of an international membership of science, natural history, art, architecture, applied arts and science, history, and children's museums; soos and aquariums; and playwrights, directors and performers.

IMTAL is overseen by an Executive Director and nine member multi-national board of directors, representing a full spectrum of museums.

WHAT IS MUSEUM THEATRE?

IT'S EDUCATIONAL!

The fusion of the seemingly disparate disciplines of theatre, education, art, history, and science has a very long history. Using theatre as an educational tool has its roots in ancient Greek theatre, where performances included religious and historic references, as well as entertainment.

IT'S EFFECTIVE!

First used by only a few pioneering institutions, theatre in museums has grown into a full-fledged movement. Innovative museum professionals around the world have turned to theatre as a successful medium for educating visitors, and evaluation studies have shown its effectiveness.

IT CAN WORK FOR YOU!

The stylistic elements of museum theatre continue to evolve, from storytelling and living history, to mime and puppetry, to comedy and musical. Each museum must find the theatre forms which best suit its educational goals and museum facilities, and through work with theatre professionals, develop its own unique theatre program.

JOIN IMTAL AND RECEIVE...

PUBLICATIONS

- Subscription to IMTAL INSIGHTS, a quarterly newsletter containing articles by museum and theatre professionals.

- Discount on cooperative publications, such as

Perspectives on Museum Theatre, a resource report of evaluations and articles, developed with the American Association of Museums.

• *Annual Resource Directory*, detailing IMTAL members programs & productions, and script listings, plus consultants.

VALUABLE INFORMATION

• Letter and telephone referrals, for museums and artists.

• Support for start-up programs.

• Access to proven scripts and theatre program structures.

OPPORTUNITIES TO COME TOGETHER

• Annual meeting during AAMs Annual Conference.

• IMTAL has presented sessions at over 25 regional, national, and international conferences.

• Future seminars and workshops on subjects related to museum theatre, such as evaluation and styles.

• Script exchanges and touring productions.

MEMBERSHIP CATEGORIES (check one)

❏   Full-time student $15

❏   Individual Professional $35

❏   Institutions/Company $75

MEMBERSHIP FORM

Date_____

To become a member, submit this completed form and mail to IMTAL with check payable to Museum of Science (include on check: IMTAL membership) and mail to:

IMTAL
Museum of Science
Science Park
Boston, MA 02114-1099.

_____
Name/Contact

_____
Institution

_____
Position/Title

_____
Address

_____
Clity/State/Zlip

_____
Province/Country

_____
Telephone/Fax

_____
E-Mail

Note that IMTAL memberships are on a yearly renewal basis, from September-August

APPENDIX B

MUSEUM THEATER POSITION DESCRIPTION

TITLE: Theater Director or Coordinator

REPORTS TO: Education VP/Curator or Visitor Services or Collection Curator

POSITION OBJECTIVE: To manage the institution's theater program.

PRIMARY DUTIES:

- Manage the institution's theater program including hiring, supervision, script development, stage design and construction, prop design and construction, show scheduling.

- Coordinate programming and scheduling with other program coordinators throughout the institution.

- Develop shows and programs that support the institution's mission and educational philosophy.

- Serve as Guardian of content accuracy by soliciting feedback on show theme and content from curators and other interested and involved parties.

- Evaluate all shows through written, objective studies and reviews. Seek peer review (internally and externally) and feedback on measurement instruments.

- Develop annual and long-term strategic plans for theater's place within the institution.

- Manage budget.

QUALIFICATIONS:

- One to two years experience directing theatrical performances.

- Experience conducting auditions and casting actors.

- Ability to coach and work with a wide variety of people a must.

- Creativity in program design critical for success.

- Must possess ability to alter show content and theme as necessary and required by supervisor.

- Improvisational skills highly preferred.

- Experience working in children's theater and/or other educational theater programs preferred.

- Ability to learn, interpret, and share the purpose of the institution and its collection.

- Ability to quickly adapt to changing conditions and respond professionally.

- Must possess the desire and ability to be flexible.

- Outstanding interpersonal skills with the ability to work with a variety of people.

- Ability to organize workload, self, and subordinates.

MUSEUM THEATER POSITION DESCRIPTION

TITLE: Stage Manager

REPORTS TO: Theater Coordinator or Director

POSITION OBJECTIVE: To oversee and manage all technical aspects of show/theater production.

PRIMARY DUTIES:

• Oversee all aspects of stage preparation, construction, and maintenance of staging areas.

• Coordinate staging needs (e.g., space, lighting, and signage) in cooperation with the institution's operations and/or grounds department(s).

• Prepare staging area for daily shows and presentations. Adjusts lighting, signage, or other needs as required by the theater department and show.

• Maintain clean and attractive show areas during show times as well as off-performance times.

QUALIFICATIONS:

• Strong technical skills with experience in lighting, construction, and or general maintenance preferred.

• Experience with theatrical staging a plus.

• Strong ability to use most standard tools and repair a variety of materials, props, and other items a must.

• Good interpersonal skills with the ability to work with a variety of people.

• Ability to work flexible hours, including weekends as necessary.

MUSEUM THEATER POSITION DESCRIPTION

TITLE:	Actor
REPORTS TO:	Theater Coordinator or Director
POSITION OBJECTIVE:	To perform high quality structured and improvisational shows for the purpose of educating and entertaining visitors to our facility.

PRIMARY DUTIES:

- Learn new material for the purpose of presenting new shows and programs.

- Contribute to the creation of shows and programs performed.

- Adjust performance as required by the director or other institutional staff.

- Respond to and incorporate direction offered by theater director or coordinator.

- Maintain flexibility in workday in order to adjust to changing visitor needs (e.g., change show schedule to meet attendance needs for the day).

QUALIFICATIONS:

- Experience working in children's theater and/or other educational theater programs preferred.

- Ability to learn, interpret, and share the purpose of the institution and its collection.

- Ability to quickly adapt to changing conditions and respond professionally.

- Must possess the desire and ability to be flexible.

- Improvisational skills a plus.

- Good interpersonal skills with the ability to work with a variety of people.

- Ability to work flexible hours, including weekends as necessary.

APPENDIX C

GLENBOW REMINISCENCE KITS

REMINISCENCE KITS ARE MINI-MUSEUMS IN SUITCASES DESIGNED FOR OLDER ADULTS.

KIT # 1:   SUGAR AND SPICE: MEMORIES OF BAKING

Baking recalls sweet memories of home made aromatic with spices, warmed with oven heat, and the promise of good things to eat. Baking recalls home-baked breads, pies, cakes, and special pastries baked for the holidays and special occasions. And all these riches were created with a few simple kitchen implements, a favourite recipe, and a loving pair of hands.

KIT # 2:   SALAD DAYS: COOKING UP MEMORIES

Before convenience foods made their mark, meal-making often required elaborate preparation in the kitchen. It was hard work. Foods had to be chopped, mashed, ground, grated, sieved, and pounded by hand with the help of kitchen gadgets. Sometimes there was an extra pair of hands in the kitchen - hired help, or daughters, however unwillingly recruited from their play.

KIT # 3:   A LITTLE DAB 'LL DO YA: ACCESSORIES FOR MEN

Remember the TV commercial, Brylcream, A little dab 'll do ya, Brylcream, You look so debonair, in the 50s? Or reading the Burma-Shave signs along the highways in the 40s? Stopping at the barber's for a shave and a haircut, and at the shoe shine stand for a spiffy polish? A close shave or a favourite pipe is a comfort, a moment of relaxation in a workaday world. Moments like these can be enjoyed in solitude, or shared with friends.

KIT # 4:   IN THE PINK: GROOMING MEMORIES FOR WOMEN

Looking good is feeling good. Memories of "putting on your face" recall those private hours in the beauty parlour or at the dressing table at home. Sweet-smelling powders, creams, and perfumes, hair freshly washed and curled - all help to put your best face forward to meet the day.

KIT # 5:   ON THE TOWN: DRESS-UP FOR MEN

Memories of going to town, whether for business or pleasure, recall a favourite hat or tie, perhaps a clean collar or pair of sock garters, or even spats to achieve a dressy look.

KIT # 6:   DRESSED TO THE NINES: DRESS-UP FOR WOMEN

Remember when women rarely appeared in public without a hat and gloves? Putting on a new hat is like putting on a new face, a new mood. A hat can give you pizzazz, a light and lively look, or a dignified and solemn air. With purse and freshly-laundered gloves, and a fur for dressy occasions, you can meet the world knowing you look your very best.

KIT # 7:   SCHOOL SPIRIT

School days…the rush to get to school before the bell rang. The long, slow afternoons dragging on forever. A special teacher who made learning a delight - or a nightmare. The strap. The games played during recess, the school concert, and the school dance. Perhaps best of all, playing on the winning team which brought home the championship trophy.

KIT #8:REMEMBERING THE WAR

Memories of the Second World War... Dieppe, D-Day, Hiroshima. The Red Cross, the RCAF on bomber runs over Germany, and U-Boats in the North Atlantic. On the radio, Winston Churchill, the Happy Gang, Benny Goodman, and the Andrews Sisters singing Don't sit under the apple tree/ With anyone else but me. On the home front, women working in the Ogden shops, coping with ration coupons, and selling Victory Bonds. And at the end of the war, the troops coming home at last.

KIT # 9:   MUSIC, GAMES, AND FUN

It feels good to relax with friends or family at home. It's all about singing songs around a piano, or friendly competition in a game of cards or Monopoly. On the radio, you might tune into a comedy or variety show, a mystery serial, big band swing, or a catchy radio jingle. Or you might show snapshots from the last trip to the Rocky Mountains, or the latest finds for your stamp collection.

KIT # 10:   BABY OF MINE

There is so much to do for a new baby - feed baby, change baby, bathe and powder, and just cuddle baby. Nursery rhymes, peek-a-boo, and pat-a-cake games, and lullabies at bedtime. Think of your baby peacefully asleep, playing with a special toy, teething, squalling. There are the baby's first smile, tooth, word, and wobbly steps to celebrate.

KIT # 11:   GIRLS' PLAY

When you're a little girl, a favourite doll is something you can tell your secrets to. You keep your tiny treasures in a special little box, with a lock and key. With your friends, you can play ring-around-a-rosy, hopscotch, or dress up in grownup clothes. You help mother around the house, or practise baking on a toy stove, or sewing clothes for your doll. And in quiet moments, a favourite storybook or book of fairy tales takes you to faraway lands.

KIT # 12:   TOYS FOR BOYS

When you're a little boy, it seems as if the whole world out there is waiting to be discovered. There are toys and games to be tried and mastered. With some nails and scrap wood, you can build a kingdom - or at least a playhouse with your friends. A blade of grass makes a good whistle; two tin cans and a string can be turned into a telephone. In wintertime, snow is for sledding and rolling into snowballs and snow forts; ice is for skating and dreaming of your hockey hero.

The Glenbow Museum's Reminiscence Kits are available for loan for 14-day periods: $25 for a single loan. $195 for a Ten-Loan Special. (Fee includes GST.)

The borrower assumes the cost and responsibility of transportation to and from Glenbow's loading dock (819-1st Street S.E., Calgary, Alberta, Canada).

To book, please call (403) 268-4110.

APPENDIX D

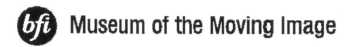

(MOMI) INFORMATION LEAFLET
(sent to applicants)

MUSEUM OF THE MOVING IMAGE
ACTORS' COMPANY

Thank you for your interest in applying for a position with the Actors' Company.

Actors in MOMI are first-person interpreters who work on their own in two areas on alternate weeks. The research the social and film history of two areas using prepares research material, books, films and video, and attending seminars. Once cast, actors devised their own characters working in small groups with the director. These characters will interact with the public, give information, entertain, demonstrate exhibits and commentate on films.

The locations are: Victorian (Pre-Cinema), Edwardian Electric Palace, Hollywood Casting Office c. 1928, Soviet Agit-Prop Train, Hollywood Studio 1939, and Odeon Cinema 1946.

Our aim is provide an elite team of motivated professionals, so please read these notes on recruitment procedure. We try to make the group auditions as enjoyable as possible to reflect the enjoyment that working at MOMI brings. Working here is a training in itself, and most actors gain increased confidence, a greater awareness of strengths in their performance and personal resources and an ability to work generously as part of a large team.

Working as an actor in MOMI is not a casual "holiday" job, nor a job for "out of work" actors. It is a total commitment to maintain the highest standards of theatre in museum performance, and keep MOMI at the forefront of this exciting medium.

STRUCTURE OF COMPANY

Actors are engaged on a fixed short term contract, which includes a three-week rehearsal period. Each actor plays two characters, alternating from week to week. There are three shifts of six actors and one animator. Everyone works on a two-day on, one day off rota throughout the contract, either on a 9:30-3:30 or a 12-6 shift. The Museum is open seven days a week.

Each actor works on his or her own in their designated area except in the Odeon where two actors work together.

No actor may stay on for a further contract, but may apply again in the future. Since the Museum opened in 1988 many actors have returned, some for several contracts. Ex actors are encouraged to work in different areas, and are not automatically taken on again.

TRAINING

The three week rehearsal period is carefully structured to provide seminars and practical sessions with appropriated experts, screenings, and improvisation and character work with the director. Disability awareness and health and safety matters are also included. Some early morning and evening rehearsals are scheduled.

AUDITIONS

Group auditions are held three times a year. Between twelve and twenty people are invited to one of five sessions. The first hour and a half consist of a series of impro games, after which a number of the auditionees will be released, Those remaining will stay on to perform a pre-prepared speech and do some further impro work.

The director and company manager will then select which actors will return for a recall interview. Those reaching this stage will return within a few days to find out more about the job and be asked in greater detail about their interest in working at MOMI.

The contracts with the acting company are not Equity status as we do not wish to limit our choice in attracting a wide range of skills. It is not a strictly theater job – an ex-teacher with drama training would potentially be an ideal candidate.

We strive to employ an equal mix of men and women, of varying ages – most actors are in their late 20's and early 30's. We have no prejudice with regard to older actors (several actors in their 60's have worked with us) but we do extend caution to those under 23 years. This is because working constantly with the public demands a high level of maturity and ability to take decisions. Each person effectively works alone and unsupervised with responsibility not only for entertainment and information, but also customer care and health and safety.

WHAT WE ARE LOOKING FOR

Our commitment to excellence means that we spend a lot of time to find the right people for the Actors' Company. You will need to demonstrate a totally professional integrity to research and an enthusiasm to work directly with the public including children and those with learning difficulties.

You will have stamina and high energy, be good with people and enjoy communicating your passion for the stories behind the development of the moving image. You will also be able to display a person generosity of spirit with an ability to listen. Good improvisation and communication skills are thus vital together with the experience to create "real" characters.

A degree on A levels are important to us as they show that you have the necessary skills for study and the academic background to absorb prodigious amounts of information.

You will also have a positive and mature attitude to punctuality and attendance and show a desire to maintain fitness throughout the contract.

HOW TO APPLY

- Respond to our advert in The Stage or PRC.
- Write a short letter telling us why you would like to work at MOMI
- Your CV should show your training and academic qualifications, your age and any teaching or other relevant experience. Acting CVs which are simply lists of theatre or TV credits are of minimal interest to us.
- We are keen to see languages (especially Russian) and need to know of you have interests in film or history. These are not essential but might help your application.
- Enclose a recent photograph.
- Be aware of the work involved and how you feel you could contribute to our high standards.
- Enclose a SAE large enough for the return of you photograph. We receive a large number of applications and do not have the resources to write out hundred of envelopes. If you are not offered an audition and have not enclosed an SAE, any reply will take low priority owing to the pressures of auditioning. We do not pay fares or expenses to auditions.

Andrew Ashmore
Company Manager

Julia Munrow
Director

SUMMARY OF RESEARCH PACK AND REHEARSALS FOR PRE-CINEMA CHARACTER (1986)

MUSEUM OF THE MOVING IMAGE.

ACTORS' COMPANY

ACTORS RESEARCH MATERIAL:

(Example of Pre-Cinema character, 1896)

RESEARCH PACK

Part I:

Notes on the area

Reference Book List

Education Leaflet: "The First Moving Pictures"

Key Facts—A genealogy of the cinema

Chronological summary and basic social history information

Extract from "A Social History of England" by Asa Briggs

Two-page article on the Fantasmagorie

Explanations of Thaumatrope, Phenakistoscope, Zoetrope, Praxinioscope, Birth of Photography, Wet and Fry Plate Photography, Chronophotography, Zoopraxiscope , Photographic Gun, Magic Lantern, Theatre Optique (and French lyrics to original song), Kinetoscope, and Mutoscope

Articles on the History and Origins of Photography (35 pages)

Articles on Eadweard Muybridge and Emile Reynaud

Article on Early British Photographers

"The Art of the Daguerreotype" (Exhibition leaflet, Getty Museum, Los Angeles)

Part II:

Articles on the Fantasmagorie and other early magic lantern shows (20 pages)

Extracts From the Magic Lantern Journal (10 pages)

Information on the Lumiere Brothers and a contemporary record of their first London shows (10 pages)

Filming the Derby

Extract from 300 years of Cinematography

Facsimile Magic Lantern Advertisements

**THE ACTORS' PREPARATION SESSIONS FOR
PRE-CINEMA OVER A THREE-WEEK PERIOD INVOLVE:**

Initial introduction session	3 hours
Research preparation sessions and introduction to the library	
Character work with the actors' company director	10 hours
Lectures on:	

Magic Lanterns	1.5 hours
Muybridge, Marey and Edison's Kinetoscope	1.5 hours
Emile Reynaud and the Theatre Optique	1.5 hours
The Lumiere Brothers and the Cinematographe	1.5 hours
Hands-on practical Seminar on Victorian Printmaking	3 hours
Screening of viewing materials	2 hours

Practical Training on how to operate the Magic Lantern and Theatre Optique
Disability Awareness session
Museum Operations and Health and Safety Training
Education Department Briefing on School Visits

Costume Meeting and Fitting
Photoshoot

Rehearsal for KS2 performance workshops —"Entertaining athe Victorians"

Each actor plays two characters.

MUSEUM OF THE MOVING IMAGE

GUIDELINES

To do this work successfully you have to be in an absolutely positive frame of mind all of the time.

The characters you will crate will be extrovert characters.

Your objective is to bring the museum to life.

You will have to know your area, fall in love with it and communicate your passion for it to the visitor so that there would be a fundamental lack of you weren't there.

You have to find ways of involving people, individuals, and groups who come in their hundreds of thousands from all over the planet to visit the museum. People of all ages, races, nationalities, people with disabilities,. People who don't understand you, who can't hear you, who can't see you. People who are shy, people with fond memories, experts, students, serious people, playful people...

They will all have different needs, desires and expectations. Some will be here for hours. Some will rush through but in the end they come to a museum for knowledge.

They will get it in a variety of ways from you—chats, lectures, entertainment and play. Explanations., stories, anecdotes, gossip, jokes, songs, demonstrations and sometimes a bit of conflict.

To ensure the authenticity of the period, you have to do EVERYTHING IN CHARACTER.

To be IN CHARACTER you have to know the social, economic. Political circumstance of your period: the religious, sexual, familial values of that time; the class background and the particular demands of the job/role that you depict. It is absolutely essential that you capture, in detail, the linguistic and physical life of the character in his/her period and are able to maintain that throughout your interaction with the public. That is the challenge and that is the fun!

So, while you are reading, have all that at the front of your mind.

Information has to be researched. The more you know the more fun you can have.

Make notes, but not so many that you have to re-research your notes.

If you get bored reading. Stop; make notes on what interests you.

Different locations in the museum do have different demands. These are indicated on the following pages. (ed. note: these pages not included here)

Remember—your research doesn't stop at the end of the three-week rehearsal—its only just begun.

APPENDIX E

NOTES ON CONTRIBUTORS

MICHAEL ALEXANDER is the program manager of Live Presentations and Science Theater at the Boston Museum of Science. He received a Bachelors degree in Physics from Bates College and has used that training to develop methods to enhance performances with electronics, mechanics, and optics. In the mid 1980s he helped inaugurate a theater program at the Boston Museum of Science to deal with issues and subjects that were difficult to present using more traditional museum methods. He also developed the Theater of Electricity at the museum featuring the world's largest air-insulated Van de Graaff generator.

ANDREW ASHMORE read Law and Criminology before admitting his desire to pursue a career in acting. After a brief spell as an advertising copywriter to fund drama training, his first professional job was in a Museum as part of the Museum of the Moving Image (MOMI) Actors' Company. Two years as an actor/interpreter with Action Replay at the National Museum of Photography, Film and Television was followed by further contracts with MOMI, and a number of freelance Museum-based projects. He became Manager of the MOMI Actors' Company in December 1996, and is currently working to establish International Museum Theater Alliance (IMTAL)-Europe to develop communication between Museums and actors.

SHELI BECK is the Executive Director of Living History at The Astors' Beechwood Mansion – Victorian Living History Museum in Newport, Rhode Island. She has a background as a theatrical performer, designer, playwright, and acting coach. At Beechwood since 1989, Sheli has created an internship for young actors, as well as the Victorian Christmas Feast. She credits the success of the museum to the hardworking and creative production staff. Sheli joined the board of directors of IMTAL in 1998. Originally from St. Louis, she now resides in Portsmouth, RI, with the love of her life, Tom.

TESSA BRIDAL is Director of Public Programs for the Science Museum of Minnesota, where the use of theater was pioneered almost 30 years ago. She founded and conducts the annual Theater in Museums Workshop, now in its 14th year. Philadelphia Zoo Treehouse staff have attended the Workshop since 1996, and been part of the Workshop's Guest Presenter Series for several years. Bridal is also chair of the American Association of Museum's (AAM) Museum Theater Professional Interest Council, which twice a year publishes a journal of in-depth articles submitted by museum theater practitioners. In 1994, Bridal won AAM's Education Committee's Award for Excellence for her work in museum theater.

SHERRY ANNE CHAPMAN is responsible for programming for older adults at the Glenbow Museum in Calgary, Alberta, Canada where she has been since 1994. As part of her Master of Museum Studies program focusing on live interpretation, she spent a three-month internship in 1993 at Colonial Williamsburg in Virginia.

LYNNE CONNER, PH.D., is a theater and dance historian and a free-lance playwright living and working in Pittsburgh, Pennsylvania. She currently teaches theater history at Carnegie Mellon University and was for three years the Director of Stages in History, the resident professional theater company of the Heinz History Center. Her plays and translations have been produced by a variety of professional and museum theater companies.

WENDY ELLEFSON is the Interpretive Programs Manager at the Minnesota Historical Society's History Center in Saint Paul. During her 11 years with the Society she has performed, researched, developed, and managed a wide variety of interpretive programs. Her recent museum theater projects include Manoominikewin: A Wild Ricing Puppet Show and Lifting as We Climb: African American Women Working for Change. She is currently developing a theater program for the upcoming exhibit, Tales of the

Territory: Minnesota 1849 - 1858. She has a B.A. in history from the University of Minnesota and a healthy respect for the lively art and delicate craft of drama.

BOB FINTON started his involvement with informal science education in July of 1988 and quickly made use of museum theater as a unique and fun teaching tool. Ha has written and performed in several pieces with a wide range of topics and a variety of presentation styles. The Maryland Science Center, in Baltimore's Inner Harbor, has been host to single-actor plays about biology, complex presentations regarding paleontology, and elaborate productions detailing the physics of stage special effects. Of all the hard lessons learned, Bob has come to realize that museum theater needs fun, flexibility, and a good professional director.

ANN FORTESCUE is Director of Education at the Historical Society of Western Pennsylvania and current chair of the Mid-Atlantic Association of Museums Educators Committee. Ann participated in planning and opening the Senator John Heinz Pittsburgh Regional History Center and led the team developing "Discovery Place," a low-tech, hands-on exhibit for children and adults. Ann is involved in program development and evaluation, training education staff., volunteers, and interns, creating program budgets, and this year managing the History Center's MAP III grant. She serves on the Pennsylvania Historical Association's Council and has served on the board of the Pennsylvania Council for Social Studies. Ann has been a museum educator in historic houses and history museums in Massachusetts and New York. She holds a B.A. in history from Bates College and an M.S. in Museum Education from Bank Street College of Education.

KEVIN FRISCH has been building and performing puppet shows professionally since 1986, the year he began working with a permanent marionette theater located in Brooklyn, New York, The Puppetworks Inc. There he performed six days a week, two and sometimes three shows a day for nine years. In 1995 he relocated back to his hometown of Cincinnati, Ohio and opened The Frisch Marionette Company. He occasionally builds puppets for

collectors, TV or magazine ads and since 1994, has designed and built hand puppets, masks, and full body costumes for theatrical and educational productions of The Central Park Wildlife Center in New York City.

JOHN FULWEILER has been a professional actor for several years in New York City. Mr. Fulweiler began his work for the Wildlife Conservation Society at the New York Aquarium, where he created "Dr. Coates" an improvisational, interactive character who performed experiments in the Fish That Go Zap exhibit. He later worked for three years as the Theater Coordinator for the Central Park Zoo where he created the current Wildlife Theater and Acorn Theater programs, and developed environmental characters which appear throughout the zoo.

A graduate from the University of California at Santa Barbara in Political Science and from the University of Georgia with a Master's degree in Public Policy and Administration, **AMY GROFF** has been involved in the field of informal education for over eight years. She began her career in humane education in the Washington, DC area, and worked at Zoo Atlanta where she held a number of rewarding educational positions over a span of five years. Recently she took a position as Curator of Education for Cast Programs on the opening team with Disney's Animal Programs in the division of Conservation and Science at Disney's Animal Kingdom. Of notable professional interest to Amy in zoo education is the use of theater in public programming, animal management, and keeper training as well as in adult education.

PROF. GEORGE E. HEIN was founding director of the Ph.D. Program and the Program Evaluation Research Group (PERG) at Lesley College, both of which have contributed to museum education and visitor studies. He has served as both secretary and chair of the International Council of Museums' (ICOM) International Committee on Education and Cultural Action, and is a member of the AAM/ICOM Board, AAM Education Committee and the Committee on Audience Research, and of the Visitor Studies Association.. He is the author of Learning in the Museum (Routledge, 1998), and, with Mary Alexander, Museums: Places of Learning, (AAM, 1998).

CATHERINE HUGHES is an actor, director and writer, who has practiced theater at the Museum of Science in Boston for more than ten years. She coordinates the Science Theater Program there and is founder and Executive Director of the IMTAL, a nonprofit membership organization and an Affiliate to the AAM. She is the author of *Museum Theater: Communicating with Visitors through Drama.* In addition to speaking at numerous national and international conferences, Hughes has guest lectured at museum studies programs at Harvard, Tufts and Cooperstown.

JULIE JOHNSON is Director of Education for the New Jersey State Aquarium where she oversees the design and implementation of public, family and school programs and exhibits. She is project director and principal investigator for a number of programs of which the Philadelphia/Camden Informal Education Collaborative Family Learning Project, and the Camden Aquarium Urban Science Enrichment programs are most notable. She serves on the board of Trustees of the New Jersey Association of Museums and is a member of several professional organizations including the National Science Teachers Association, Association for Women in Science, AAM and ASTC.

DALE JONES, Senior Associate at the Institute for Learning Innovation, designs materials and programs, conducts research and evaluation, and coordinates professional development at the Institute. He has created museum theater, living history, hands-on, and interpretive experiences for a variety of museums and organizations. He was formerly Director of Interpretation at the Baltimore City Life where he brought to life galleries and historic homes, creating museum theater focusing on the lives of African-Americans in the 19th Century while exploring characters as diverse as Captain John Smith, early settlers of the frontier, and H. L. Mencken.

JON LIPSKY is an Associate Professor of playwriting and acting at Boston University's School for the Arts. Since 1988 he has been the principle playwright for Boston's Museum of Science, having scripted and directed over a dozen plays. His professional work has been seen in numerous regional theaters, including the Actor's Theater of Louisville, which chose one of his plays for the prestigious Humana Festival in 1994. He is also the Associate Artistic Director of The Vineyard Playhouse, the professional theater on Martha's Vineyard, where he lives year-round with his wife, Kanta, and sons, Adam and Jonah.

TRACY MACMORINE coordinates the Cast Theater Program at the Cincinnati Museum Center, where, over the past four years she has produced 32 shows – 29 of which she also directed, 22 of which she also wrote. Tracy has a B.F. A. in acting and has completed graduate work in directing at the University of Cincinnati's College Conservatory of Music. A strong advocate for theater as an educational tool, she served as artistic director of Players from the Heart, a theater troupe comprised of adults surviving mental illness whose mission was to educate by demystifying the struggles and triumphs involved with this disease and its recovery. She also spent a year as artist-in-residence at an elementary school, working with K-5th grade teachers and their students to develop a comprehensive, academically integrated creative dramatics curriculum for each grade level.

LAURA MALONEY was introduced to the museum theater concept at the Philadelphia Zoo in 1987 while interning for the Treehouse program. In 1991, as Curator of Education for the new Aquarium of the Americas in New Orleans, she experimented with theater as a public programming tool. Shortly thereafter, with her theatrical programming skills honed, Laura was recruited to develop and launch a high-profile theater program at the Central Park Zoo in New York City. Laura is a past board member of IMTAL.

CHRISTY S. MATTHEWS is the Director of Program Development for the Colonial Williamsburg Foundation. She is responsible for all daily programming in the Historic Area. From 1994-1997 she served as Director of African American Interpretation and Presentations before being named Director of Midtown Programs and Operations. She continues to oversee African American programs, but adds to the list, Women's Studies, Religious Studies, Character Interpretation Development, Seasonal and Special Programs.

SUSAN MCLEOD O'REILLY has worked in a variety of positions in Canadian museums over the past two decades. For many years she conducted research, acquired artifacts and curated exhibitions in her role as curator at the National Postal Museum. From there she moved to overseeing the development of exhibitions and programs at the Postal Museum. Currently, as head of interpretive programs at the Canadian Museum of Civilization, Susan manages the development of interpretive products and programs, including theater, at Canada's most visited museum. Susan worked for several years as archaeologist before undertaking formal studies in museology.

SIMONE MORTAN has worked for the past three years as a Visitor Programs Specialist at the Monterey Bay Aquarium. She began her career in natural history interpretation in 1976 with East Bay Regional Parks in Berkeley, California. After returning to the Monterey Bay area in 1981, she worked independently as a project coordinator for the Land Trust of Santa Cruz County, an artist in the schools (storyteller and fiber artist) and a freelance naturalist. One career highlight included work with school children for the successful construction and launch of an Ohlone Indian style tule canoe.

HARRY NEEDHAM has been a professional evaluator for more than 20 years and has directed/conducted almost 100 studies, many of them at the Canadian Museum of Civilization and Canadian War Museum. He developed a "do-it-yourself" approach for evaluation that has attracted the interest of institutions in several countries. He is member of the editorial board of the Canadian Journal of Program Evaluation and has lectured extensively and conducted workshops on evaluation, visitor studies and live interpretation in the U.S., Canada, Australia, and New Zealand. In a few months, he will devote all his time to consulting.

ROBERT A. RICHTER, a founder of AAM's Museum Theater Professional Interest Council, was on staff at Mystic Seaport for over ten years, where he was responsible for the development and supervision of theater, music and first-person interpretation programs. Mr. Richter has also served as a consultant for performance-based programs at numerous museums in New England. In addition to museum work, he is an actor, director and producer of theater and video productions. Currently, Mr. Richter is on staff at Connecticut College where he oversees programming for the College's Arts Initiative.

KATHLEEN F. WAGNER is Senior Vice President for Education at the Philadelphia Zoo, where her responsibilities include interpretation, group programs, and oversight of the Children's Zoo and award-winning experiential children's center, the Treehouse. She co-founded the Zoo's Education Department in 1976, and has served in a number of management roles. Ms. Wagner has consulted with zoos, museums, and aquariums throughout the country, and was instrumental in the development of the New Jersey State Aquarium. Ms. Wagner's particular interest is in conservation interpretation for family audiences, and the use of theater in zoos. She has presented papers at numerous national conferences and co-authored three publications on family learning and family activity kits. She is a graduate of Bucknell University, and has a master's degree from Villanova University.

APPENDIX F

GLOSSARY OF TERMS

MUSEUM THEATRE: umbrella term used to describe a variety of theatrical forms taking place in a museum, zoo or aquarium, as well as outreach programs attached to such institutions.

FIRST-PERSON INTERPRETATION: an interpreter who takes on a character, usually from another time in history; speakes in first-person

COSTUMED INTERPRETATION: any interpretation done in costume; can be first- or third-person interpretation, or museum theatre.

THIRD-PERSON INTERPRETATION: an interpreter who interprets a time-period, but does not take on the role of another character; does not speak in first-person

LIVING HISTORY: interpreting the past through costumed interpretation and characters, demonstration of historical processes, and reenactment of past events.

RESIDENT THEATRE COMPANY: a group of theatre professionals hired as museum staff who create organic theatre pieces designed for the museum's exhibits and programs.

REMINISCENCE THEATRE: A play or other dramatic performance that is developed directly from the memories of older adults surrounding a defined theme and that is intended to awaken memories, entertain, and spark further discussion amongst the audience and the actors. This type of theatre can serve a therapeutic purpose through the valuing of memories through the collection of the reminiscences in developing the play and through the sharing of new memories that occurs after each performance. The process in which a person's memories are shared, heard, and valued can result in a renewed sense of self.